Anatomy  of a Wrinkle

Fun and Inspirational Stories to Help Smooth Out the Wrinkles of Life

RuthKay Petersen

POWERPRESS PUBLISHING

GREENWOOD VILLAGE, CO

First Edition

Library of Congress Control Number: 2001 130083
1. Inspiration   2. Self-Help

ISBN: 0-9708149-0-9

Editors: Ann Marie Gordon
                 Michel duBois Petersen
Illustrator: Jeff McClung
Book Design: Paulette Livers
Photographer: Eric Weber

POWERPRESS PUBLISHING
8547 E. Arapahoe Rd., No. J190
Greenwood Village, CO 80112

Contents

Contents

Acknowledgments

My mother, Ruth G. "Pat" Spears, was a Registered Nurse. Her mother told her at an early age that when she grew up she must pursue a nursing career. Although she was a wonderful and dedicated nurse, I could tell by our many conversations that my mother's desire was to become a dancer, an artist, and a writer; however, her parents thought her dreams were nonsense. I am so very grateful to my mother for letting me live my dreams by providing me with dancing, acting, and baton lessons, plus encouragement because they were the foundation for helping me achieve my goals today.

Whenever I hear Bette Midler sing *The Wind Beneath My Wings*, I am always reminded of my best friend, Shirley Eckert. She is the wind beneath my wings. Shirley has helped me survive tough times in my personal life and business and has helped make this book become a reality.

After hearing Bobbi Sims speak at the Crystal Cathedral in Garden City, California, attending her workshops, and reading her books, she became my lifetime role model. Her wisdom and spiritual guidance has enriched my life immensely.

To write this book, it took many hours on the computer. The computer has always been my enemy. If it were not for Paula Jean Pevc helping me with my computer skills and getting me out of some real jams, this book might not have been released for another 20 years!

Two extremely gifted editors, Ann Marie Gordon and Michel deBois Petersen, have been a real blessing. Their knowledge, honesty, encouragement and editing skills helped my dream of writing this book come true.

A very special thanks to Elaine Dumler, Mary Kay McCarthy and Jennifer McCarthy for their support and critiques.

My sincere thanks and appreciation to Jeffrey McClung for helping my stories come alive with his illustrations.

I am very grateful to Paulette Livers for doing such a magnificent job in the book's design.

A heartfelt thanks to my precious son, Darrin Petersen. His sense of humor kept me laughing.

Anatomy
of a
Wrinkle

INTRODUCTION

When I get up in the morning, I always seem to sleepwalk for the first five minutes. I stumble around my bedroom, yawn and stretch my way to the bathroom. I do love my spacious bathroom, especially with its big oval tub, because regardless of how much weight I gain I still fit in it. One morning, however, as I staggered down the hallway with my slippers scuffling, I had an unforgettable awakening.

Once in the bathroom I flipped on the light switch and gazed in the mirror at my pajama-clad self and my blonde "bed head" framing my sleepy face. I looked again at myself in the mirror and suddenly had a life-changing experience. You see, my bathroom has wall-to-wall mirrors and at this disgustingly early hour of the morning and under the blaze of stark and unforgiving electric lights, this "House-of-Mirrors" effect really jolted me wide-awake! I could not ignore what I saw reflecting back at me. I turned from the front of my vanity cabinet to the mirror on the right of me. Ooooh! Now, to the mirror on the left. Arrghhh! Surely something is wrong with these mirrors, I thought. I just about passed out! Then I caught my breath and leaned closer to the mirror to examine what I saw. They were shining back at me in the merciless glare of the electric light—wrinkles! Hundreds of them, it seemed! Where did they come from? Was it something I ate? Was it the new cosmetics I'd been using? Oh, maybe it was the distinguished older man I'd had a date with the night before. He had thousands of wrinkles I'd thought. And then I remembered that after he brought me home last night, he gave me a peck on the cheek. That's it! Wrinkles must be contagious.

As I studied myself in those wall-to-wall mirrors, I sighed and decided to accept the newly acknowledged lines as just part of the natural aging process. It wasn't anything I had done. After all, I consoled myself, I had taken all the precautions I could to keep wrinkles at bay by using sunblock, applying moisturizers, eating properly and exercising. As I examined the wrinkles, analyzing why each one was etched into my skin, I began reflecting on the experiences of my life. The ups and downs were numerous, and it seemed like the pains and problems were like wrinkles too. Only they were wrinkles in my spirit. An abusive childhood, numerous health problems, divorce after many years of marriage, devastating personal disappointments, financial losses and the death of my beautiful daughter had caused deep lines in my heart and soul. These "wrinkles in my spirit" were not fixable by applying more moisturizer. I had to learn to attack these wrinkles with a more powerful remedy.

Writing this book has been enormously healing. As I wrote, I forced myself to revisit some of the difficult and also the memorable events in my life. Instead of looking at how bad these negative situations were, I rejoiced at how most of them had positive outcomes. By reframing my thinking, I have changed how I view my life from the past, and also how I look at my present life and my future. I really believe that if I had not revisited the past events in my life and discovered the lessons to be learned from them, some of the traumatic situations would have continued to haunt me and would negatively impact the quality of my life. This recasting has made me a much stronger person with the confidence to handle whatever life hands me. When faced with misfortunes, I immediately look for the lesson that needs to be learned. Learning that lesson helps smooth out the "wrinkles" in my life and gives me a steady sense of completeness and well being.

I discovered some of the ingredients that work for me, and they are included in the stories in this book. They are about using humor to laugh at ourselves to ease awkward moments and stressful situations, creating fun traditions that can be remembered and cherished, lessons of persistence, lessons of reflection on what I have learned in life, setting goals, overcoming challenges by adopting a positive mental attitude, nurturing self-esteem, and the rewards of a rich spiritual life.

By sharing my life stories, and the discoveries I made, my hope is that you too will be encouraged to find remedies that will help you smooth out the wrinkles that may occur in your life.

Resist reading all the stories at one time. Instead, take time to ponder each story's lesson and apply those insights to your own situations so that you may happily and hopefully create a more "wrinkle-free" life of your own.

God Bless You!

And the crowd cheered!

1

Burnt Buns

Looking into the mirror today, I not only see a lot of wrinkles, but also many fine lines, and I ask myself this question: "Just when does a 'fine line' turn into a 'wrinkle'?"

Answer: For me, it is on the occasions in my life when I have lacked the needed courage while undergoing incredible stress.

Flashback to my teenage years as a champion baton twirler: The high school band is playing and the crowd roars as I spiritedly march onto the football field for the big game. I'm dressed in a sparkly blue sequined costume and twirling two fire batons. Before all my friends and family and this huge crowd, I am in the moment I have waited for since I started twirling a baton as a young girl.

I throw my right fire baton into the night air— the firelight spinning wildly in the darkness. What a beautiful sight for all to see! After several more fancy twirls, up I throw the left baton into the air, but as I try to catch it, I trip over something on the field and I am falling down, down, down! Lunging, I catch myself and grab at the falling blazing baton, but it's too late! The ball of fire comes down and lands on me, burning my arm and one of my "buns" before it falls sizzling to the ground.

At first the crowd gasps, and then complete silence fills the stadium. My dream of doing an outstanding performance is going up in flames—all in a flash! I am humiliated and feel like such a failure before all these people. I just want to scream and run off the field.

But first I stop to think, just for a second. Yes, I could stomp off the field and wallow in the crowd's pity, or I could prove one more time to all of them and to myself that the show must go on! So, I dust myself off, pat my poor burnt bun, and pick up the flaming baton. With a deep breath I hurl it high into the air, and with my newly found confidence I toss my other baton up several more times, sending them both spinning higher and higher into the night sky. The crowd comes to their feet in one movement, erupting with cheers and whistles to show me their appreciation not only for my grand style, but more importantly, for my willingness to keep going and for not giving up!

Yes, that high school baton-twirling experience probably accounted for at least one of my first "fine lines" acquired at a very early age. But by choosing to keep my performance going, I probably smoothed out that little "fine line" before it turned into a real live "wrinkle." I call this having "courage under fire."

Tap into your courage when you're under fire!

2

Fat Chests

The summer I turned seven years old I started picking up sticks in my backyard and pretended they were batons, twirling and tossing them into the air. My mother noticed my fascination for twirling the sticks and thought maybe it was time to buy me a real baton. I remember how thrilled I was with my new baton and how I spent a tremendous amount of time and energy trying to twirl it.

The next step my mother took was to find a baton teacher for me. I will never forget my first lesson. My teacher, Delores, taught me some simple twirls, plus how to toss my baton in the air and how to catch it. Trying to follow her directions, I threw my baton up so high and so out of control that it landed in the top of a tree in the backyard. With the help of Delores's father, we retrieved my baton and we all had a good laugh at my exuberant beginnings.

Delores was also one of the most beautiful ladies I had ever seen. If you saw a picture of her, you would probably agree that she had a face like Ann-Margret and also had a figure like Dolly Parton. Delores became my idol. I wanted to look exactly like her from head to toe when I grew up.

When I became a teenager, I thought it was time for me to start developing a figure like my baton teacher's, but it just wasn't happening. I looked into the mirror and realized I was nowhere close to looking like her. The mirror became my enemy. And while all my girlfriends in junior high school had what we called "fat chests," the boys in my class referred to me as a "carpenter's dream"—flat as a board and straight as a nail.

When I was trying on my first training bra at JCPenney, the saleslady asked me, "Honey, are you sure you really need a bra?" I stood up very confidently with my chest sticking out as far as it could and I blurted out an emphatic, "Yes!" When I left the store, I knew deep down that I really didn't need a training bra because I had nothing to train. But an idea flashed into my mind and I marched straight home to the medicine cabinet where I raided my mother's supply of cotton balls and stuffed them into my new bra cups. Like magic, now I, too, suddenly had a "fat chest!"

As I grew into adulthood, everything else seemed to develop except my chest. My former husband laughingly told me to look at the bright side—I could use my itty bitty boobies as "markers" to know which side to put my bra on—front or back. Even now at my yearly mammogram exam, a team of nurses works overtime just trying to make my flat chest fit into the X-ray machine in order to take a picture. My boobs have to be stretched so far out that they resemble deflated balloons after the nurses and the machines are finished with them. It's an exhausting procedure for everyone.

I am not a quitter, though. I was still determined in my early years to look like my baton teacher, Delores. I graduated from cotton balls to padded bras, and when I wore the padded bra, I felt wonderful. "Wow! this is really something!" I thought as I turned this way and that in front of the mirror admiring my new developments.

Years later when I was scheduled to speak at a national convention with an audience of 1,000 people, I decided to wear a new "magical" bra that enhanced my figure. It was a bra that advertisers said could perform "miracles." This was a new kind of bra for me—it hooked in the front instead of in the back. (You see, I am normally a "back hooker," not a "front hooker.") I wore a close-fitting knit top and thought Dolly Parton would have been absolutely green with envy to see me in that outfit. When I walked on the stage, I smiled a big smile and opened my arms wide to greet my audience. Then my heart stopped. I had evidently failed my first attempt at mastering the art of the "front hook." The clasp had come undone and it was all too evident to the crowd what had happened. The force of the opening snap had caused my bra pads to lodge under my arms and it looked like I now had two large and two small bumps under my sweater. We (my bustline and I) were really making an entrance!

A "hush" silenced the crowd and I prayed for a laser beam to just erase me from the stage. But since I could not just excuse myself and go home, I decided I'd better turn this into a humorous situation and I said to the audience, "Well, I always wanted more, and now I have four!" The crowd roared with laughter.

What I thought of as my shortage of physical attributes, compared with those of my baton teacher and classmates, had caused me a great deal of unnecessary stress over the years.

When we continuously compare ourselves to others, we overlook all of the really wonderful qualities we possess. We will find more satisfaction by concentrating on what we DO have, not on what we DON'T have. I encourage you to write down all of your positive qualities in a journal. Review them every day to remind yourself how wonderful and special you really are.

Affirm your positive qualities every day.

🦋 3 🦋
Bad Cake Genes

My mother had excellent nursing skills and did a wonderful job taking care of her patients at the hospital where she worked. At home in the kitchen, however, her culinary skills were less than perfect. For some unknown reason her cakes never turned out well. I remember how she always hollered at them in disgust as she threw them in the trash. I know that we all inherit looks, body size, hair color, and other important characteristics from our parents, but little did I realize that the "bad cake" genes could also be inherited.

As a young bride, I wanted to learn how to bake cakes, cookies, pies—all those things that make your hips look like two battleships. After getting the recipe for lemon cake from a trusted friend, I set to work. The recipe seemed easy and I was sure my cake would be a big hit. Following the directions, I combined a lemon cake mix with the eggs it required. After a box of Lemon Jell-O was dissolved in hot water, I added it to the cake mixture. I poured the batter into the cake pan, and set the timer for 50 minutes. I was proud of myself for trying to bake something for dessert that evening.

As the cake baked, the aroma filled our small house. When the timer went off, I pulled the cake out of the oven and found that it still had liquid in the center. I called my friend Carol to ask, "Is that normal?" I'd never baked a cake before, so what did I know?

Carol said it must need a little more time to bake, and so I put the cake back in the oven for another ten minutes. It still wiggled after the ten minutes were up. "Hey, what gives?" I thought. So back in the oven it went again for another thirty minutes. A half hour later it still wasn't fully baked! After all, this wasn't exactly rocket science, so I decided against calling my friend again for more advice. I could do this on my own! I baked the cake a whole hour more. With the additional one hour and forty minutes of baking, I finally decided the cake would never be done. I don't know how I messed up the recipe, but I ended up dumping the half-baked cake in the trash, and like my mother, I hollered at it.

The cake never being done taught me that we are never done learning. Once we accept this, we can relax and enjoy the journey—even though we may not be satisfied with the outcome.

Keep learning—you are not done yet!

🦋 *4* 🦋
Get Lost!

I spent a lot of time alone after school and also during school holidays since both my parents worked full-time. I learned how to entertain myself in creative ways. Once, I set up a small museum in my bedroom which included a rock collection gathered from stones I'd found outside in the yard. Another favorite pastime of mine was selling candy in the little "candy store" that I created in the corner of my room. At Halloween, I would try to collect as much candy as possible so I could "stock" my "candy store." My family and friends would then have to buy my treats and I would end up making a few extra dollars. I was always an entrepreneur!

I also occupied my free time with dreams of becoming a famous movie star when I grew up. My mother nurtured that dream, too, by enrolling me in local theater productions. My first role was as 'Toto' in the *Wizard of Oz*. It was fun playing 'Toto.' As I crawled around the stage in my dog costume, the only things I didn't like were having to wear Kotex™ pads under my outfit to protect my knobby knees from the hardwood floor, and also having to pick up Dorothy's smelly, magic, ruby red slipper in my mouth.

I practiced my drama skills not only on stage, but also at home on the phone. I found that I was very good at imitating adult voices, so one evening when my parents went out bowling, I proceeded to call people whose names I chose at random from the phone book. Speaking in what I felt was a very sophisticated manner, I told these gullible strangers that I was a good friend and I asked them to guess who I was. When they brought up a name, I said, "That's right!" and I would also invite them over for dinner. They always seemed enthusiastic about getting together, and I knew at that moment my performance was a smash hit! After each successful phone call, I felt like a famous movie star and would run to my mirror to take a bow and throw kisses to an imaginary audience. I was having the time my life!

As the saying goes, "All good things must come to an end," and my telephone acting came to a grinding halt one day when I had the great misfortune of calling someone who worked for the telephone company. She traced my call and then contacted my mother the very next day. Mother was furious with me! Then I found myself taking another bow, but it was a different kind of a bow, as my mother gave me swats on the behind instead of applause. I learned my lesson and I never again played with calling people on the phone to invite them over for an imaginary dinner.

Even though I spent a lot of my childhood alone I learned how to entertain myself and I was never bored. Now as a single adult, I can get totally lost in things I love to do and I really enjoy my solitude. I write, dream, read, walk, observe nature, meditate and bask in the calming stillness knowing that being alone does not necessarily mean being lonely. I am always thinking of fun and creative ways to decorate my townhouse, plan a party for friends, and work on ideas for a new seminar or a book. These favorite activities help provide me with the energy I need to tackle difficult or mundane duties.

When you are feeling lonely or overwhelmed with responsibilities either at work or at home, take time out to do something you love to do. Allow yourself to "get lost" in a favorite activity and shut out the entire world.

To recharge your emotional batteries, get totally involved in something you love to do.

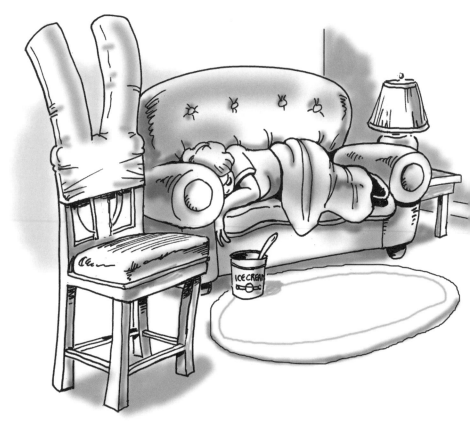

"All right, Pants, it's your turn to suffer."

❦ 5 ❦

All Stretched Out

Have you ever done something so bizarre you were ashamed of your behavior and afraid to tell someone in fear of having them think you were a few bubbles off?

I am addicted to candy, chocolate, donuts, soda pop and ice cream covered with chocolate syrup. I also love cookie dough. In my opinion the worst thing you can do to cookies is to bake them. Although I am fully aware that these goodies are full of calories, I just can't seem to resist them. After eating all these sugary calories, I always promise myself that I will exercise. For some reason, maybe a severe brain cramp, I forget to exercise plus I play a little game of denial—that I just couldn't gain weight by eating a few sweets. Well, it finally caught up with me.

I gained a few pounds—well—to be honest I gained more than a few pounds. I looked like I sat on an air hose or over-dosed on donuts. With the extra weight, my clothes were very uncomfortable, especially my pants. The elastic waistbands were extremely binding—I felt like they were squeezing the life right out of me. One afternoon I took my pants out of the washing machine and the very thought of having to wear them—having to endure the discomfort caused me to project my anger at myself on to the pants. Glaring at my pants, I stretched them over the tops of my dining room chairs thinking, "Since you were trying to strangle me, I am going to put you in the torture chamber and stretch you out and see how you like pain!"

Many health experts say that our thoughts have a big impact on our energy level and they made a believer out of me. I found myself totally exhausted, had a bowl of ice cream and rolled my chubby body onto the sofa and took a nap. When I awoke, I seemed to feel better. I stared at the chairs adorned with my pants and found myself being angry at my pants all over again. All of a sudden the famous words of my speaker-friend Bobbi Sims came to mind. In her workshops on Self-Responsibility she says that we are responsible for ourselves, our decisions, choices and actions. Something that I already knew but didn't want to admit was that the discomfort I was experiencing with my pants was not due to the elastic. It was because I allowed myself to eat uncontrollably and I had gained weight. Finally I stopped blaming my pants for being uncomfortable and I took responsibility for my poor eating habits. This prompted me to look at my life and see what other areas I was misplacing responsibility.

Never use blame to avoid responsibility.

It Could Be Worse

Every summer my parents and I went to visit my Grandpa in Kemmerer, Wyoming.

Grandpa never seemed to change. He looked the same to me when he passed away as he looked in my earliest childhood memories of him. He was about five-feet, eight inches tall, bald, slightly stooped, and always soft-spoken.

Grandpa was also a man of very few words. In fact, I don't think he said more than a total of 75 words to me in all the years I knew him. One morning as he put wood in the stove and stoked the fire, I noticed he was rubbing his back and appeared to be in pain. Concerned, I said, "Oh, Grandpa, it looks like your back is hurting." His response came in a calm voice just barely above a whisper, "It could be worse." One simple sentence—four words that have followed me throughout my life.

While living in Colorado Springs, I was running a few errands to prepare for a trip the next day. I slowed down as I approached a stoplight; but the car behind me didn't.

Crash!! "Oh, this was the last thing I needed the day before my trip," I grumbled.

"What in the world was that fellow thinking about? He was not paying attention . . . just bashed into the back of my car . . . he shouldn't even be allowed to drive . . . " my angry self clamored on and on. As often happens in difficult circumstances, my stress increased as my negative self-talk persisted.

But suddenly, a calm, familiar voice in my head replaced the agitated self-chatter. It was Grandpa's voice and it said, "It could be worse." Yes, it could be worse. No one was hurt. The car could be fixed. The world wouldn't end. Yes, it could be much worse! Thank you, Grandpa.

When bad things happen, remind yourself that it could be worse.

Hilarious Revenge

I love snoozing in the car, and whenever my former spouse (I'll refer to him as "Big L") and our kids and I would go on vacation, I would fall asleep before we got to the outskirts of town. According to my family, I was quite a sight when sound asleep in the front seat of the car. My head would be cocked to one side, my eyes rolled back in my head with just a fraction of the whites showing, and then my mouth would fall wide open. They also told me later that I snored like a freight train and I slept like a rock.

Nothing could wake me.

On one trip while I was asleep, "Big L" entertained the kids by having them tear several strips of Kleenex® and placing them one by one on the end of my tongue as he drove. With my deep, rhythmic breathing, the strips of Kleenex® stuck there and fluttered like little white flags flying in the wind. Finally, the hysterical laughter from my family woke me up. For my kids' sakes I was a good sport about it, but deep down I knew that I was going to have to figure out something equally devious and clever in order to get even with "Big L."

After having a hard day at work, "Big L" went to bed early that evening. While he slept soundly, one of his legs dangled off the bed. This was too irresistible, I thought. Slowly and stealthily I crawled next to his exposed bare foot and as I sat on the floor I delicately painted each of his toenails with bright red nail polish. The next morning the whole household awoke to the cry of a banshee! However, that was no banshee! It was my husband. "Big L" was in the shower and had apparently just discovered my artful handiwork. The kids bounded out of bed and ran into our room just in time to see their father emerge wrapped in a bath towel and dripping water all over the floor. "What the heck is this?" he demanded. He was a comical sight with shampoo suds and water streaming down his face as he hopped on his left foot and extended his right foot for us all to examine.

The kids and I held onto each other; we were laughing so hard at the absurd early morning scene. I shook my head at him and laughed and said, "I told you I'd get even with you for the Kleenex® trick!" He was naturally upset but good-natured about it and said, "Okay, you win. Now just get me some nail polish remover and get this stuff off me!" I laughed even harder when I discovered that I was out of polish remover. I offered to buy a bottle after work. He huffed and puffed and complained, while he rushed getting dressed for work.

His biggest concern was that he might have an accident that day that would force him to remove his shoes and socks. I laughed so hard my stomach hurt. It was a practical joke the whole family chuckled over for years.

Paybacks are okay if they are fun and harmless.

"HELP! What is it?"

🦋 8 🦋
Stinky Stuff

The day started out like any other. I showered, dressed, and headed to the kitchen for some breakfast. Gazing into the refrigerator I hoped something delectable would magically appear. No luck! Cereal would just have to do this morning. As I reached for the milk, something caught my eye. It was a closed leftover container near the back of the refrigerator.

I had no idea what was inside, but I peeled the lid off the plastic carton.

Wow! The odor nearly knocked me off my feet!

Oh, I wished I had a pair of those thick, elbow-length gloves worn by toxic waste handlers as I carefully placed the container on the counter. A brief family meeting was called to identify the mysterious substance in question in the plastic container, but as I suspected, no one in our household would admit they could possibly be responsible for leaving this repulsive, moldy, green cauliflower stuff in the fridge. We added this latest mystery to the long list of things we often blamed on the house "imp," who lived in our house with us. You probably have an "imp," too. You know—the same devilish little creature who hides car keys, loses the TV remote, and who eats the last brownie.

I had to hurry off to work that warm summer morning, so I just tossed the smelly container into the kitchen garbage bag and I left without another thought about it. You can imagine my horror when I returned home for lunch a few hours later and walked into a house that smelled like last year's fish catch. With my arm extended and my head tilted way back, I rushed the lethal, white kitchen bag out to the big plastic garbage can in the garage. After that distasteful task was over, I hurriedly ate a quick lunch and went back to work, satisfied I had handled a really stinky situation.

Looking back, it seems so clear what 100-degree summer temperatures would do to smelly garbage in an enclosed garage. Yet it was still a surprise (and an unpleasant one at that) when I got home that evening.

The entire garage now smelled like Hog Heaven at the petting zoo. I rushed the sack out to the big trash can outside. I thought to myself later that evening that it didn't make any difference where I put that smelly piece of cauliflower—it still caused a big stink.

My thoughts drifted to another "stinky" situation I had been dealing with at work. There was a woman named Dora whom I worked with, and who seemed to offend everyone in the office. Like the smelly, left-over cauliflower, Dora had a "stinky" attitude.

Dora was a very difficult person to work with. For one thing, she always had to be right; she was grumpy and short with people, and her outside appearance showed the exasperation she seemed to feel on the inside. There were frown wrinkles between her brows that appeared to make her face set in stone and she had a very loud and grating voice that sounded like a tuba blasting in everyone's ears all day. Several people in the office really struggled with Dora's negativity and daily put-downs.

I will have to admit that Dora was also getting under my skin. I noticed that I had begun to dread going to work because of her. Since she was draining my energy just as if she were a vampire sucking the life right out of me, I decided I must try to find a way to contend with her. On the way home after work I was listening to one of my favorite motivational speaker's inspiring cassette tapes in my car, and he said, "When people are upset or angry, they do not necessarily mean to hurt you. They themselves may be hurting." For the next week I kept replaying his message in my head and thinking about, Dora, our office "stinker."

Before leaving work one day, I went into the ladies' room and as my "favorite" co-worker was walking out, I noticed that she had been crying. Her face was splotchy and puffy and she sniffled a little as she turned away from me. Once again I heard the replay of the speaker's message in my head and I realized that maybe one of the reasons why Dora was such a challenge was because she might be depressed or sad about something. It helped me to look at her with a whole new and different perspective. It was still not easy to work with Dora, but now I was better able to cope with her behavior knowing that she must be a very sad, fearful, and wounded person.

We will always have encounters with critical, inflexible people. They are everywhere, just like the stinky odor of an old piece of cauliflower, and their negative attitudes can surely zap us like the "energy vampires." We can't wear a garlic necklace to guard ourselves from these people, but we can try to understand them and not let them affect our work performance. It is essential not to let them get us down, for their negative attitudes can be very contagious.

Create a network of positive people—those who have an upbeat view of life's trials and tribulations. Their humorous outlook will help you laugh and see the fun in life's "stinky" situations!

Hang out with positive people who have a fun sense of humor.

❦ 9 ❦

The Hair Hat

In college, I admired an upperclassman named BettyJo. In my mind, she was absolutely perfect. She was popular, beautiful, had lovely skin and flawless makeup, and she dressed fashionably. She also had a wonderful, warm personality. I was one of many underclassmen who admired BettyJo from afar on campus. Like many of my friends, I also envied and try to emulate her.

After BettyJo graduated, I didn't see her for about 10 years. One day, from out of nowhere, she called and asked if she could enroll her daughter in a baton twirling class I taught. This perfect woman whom I had admired for so long had actually called ME.

I was so flattered and excited about being able to see her again after so many years.

I invited BettyJo and her little girl, Missy, to come to the baton studio in my home the following week. I went to extremes in getting both the studio and my entire house in order. The way I agonized over the housecleaning and decorating, my family thought maybe the president of the United States would be stopping by.

I worked really hard to look perfect in BettyJo's eyes. I wanted her to notice that I had changed and even bloomed since college and that I, too, was now polished and charming—not the gawky college girl we both remembered. I improved my makeup, manicured my nails, and bought a new outfit. I even decided to have my hair trimmed.

At a nearby salon I was unfortunately assigned to a stylist who was nice, but new, and also under a lot of stress in her life. While she snipped away, she was also telling me all her troubles. She worked fast and gave me a cut so short that I was sure BettyJo would think I was losing my hair and going bald. I was in a panic about my hair—or what there was left of it! The only solution, I thought, was to wear a wig when BettyJo came over. Since my wig had been stored in a box on the closet shelf for a long time, it sort of resembled a smashed hat as I drew it out of the tissue paper.

When I first put it on and saw myself in the mirror, it looked like I was wearing a "hair hat." But what choice did I have? I thought with some styling, fluffing and some hair spray the wig would look just fine.

Well, the infamous day arrived and I was a nervous wreck, of course. I needn't have been because when BettyJo came in the door of my studio with her darling little girl, Missy, in tow she was as gracious and friendly as I'd remembered. BettyJo was still the glorious picture of smiling perfection and her daughter was a miniature replica of her mother. The baton lesson went very well and BettyJo and Missy left the studio about four. I was so pleased with myself and I just knew I had made a good impression . . . until I went to the bathroom and glanced in the mirror. What a brutal shock! Because of all the jumping and whirling around during the lesson, the front of my wig had slipped over to the side of my head, and I had bangs where I didn't want them. They weren't supposed to be over my right ear. But that wasn't the worst part!

Years before in high school, I had knocked out my front tooth while practicing my twirling and I had to wear a partial plate. Because I was so nervous that day and in a rush to answer the door, I had forgotten to put my partial plate back in my mouth after I brushed my teeth. So there I was with my crooked hair hat on and my front tooth missing. "'Well, hee-haw!' Look at me!" I groaned at my reflection in the mirror.

For the next week I kept wondering what BettyJo thought of me. Was she laughing at me or feeling sorry for me? I felt so inadequate. I felt just as I had years before when I was in school and that I would never, ever be in the big leagues in the beauty department.

To overcome my feelings of unworthiness, I thought the answer was to become perfect, not only for BettyJo, but also for everyone in my life. After all, if I didn't love myself, then how in the world could anyone else love me either? As I got older, I put a tremendous amount of effort into trying to meet my high expectations to be perfect. I spent thousands of dollars on the right cars, a model home, designer clothes, expensive cosmetics, and pricey diet programs—anything at all to help my flawed self feel perfect. For a long time, I did not realize how much stress my obsession for perfection had caused me. It took me years to realize the first person to love and approve of me, had to be me.

Today, I understand that this compulsion to be perfect was connected to my low self-esteem. Trying to be perfect is not the answer to living a happy and successful life. To feel good about myself, my work, and my contribution to the world is really the true key!

Perfect the art of feeling good about yourself.

10
Hooked at the Waist

Golden was her name. She was just like a grand-mother, sister and best friend all rolled into one person. She was a woman of wisdom; in fact, some people thought of her almost as a prophet. She loved God and was a shining, inspiring example of how to live a happy, Godly life. Her name aptly described her—she truly was "golden."

Golden also had her own beauty salon.

I met Golden when my mother took me to her salon for a manicure in preparation for my first dance recital. At the impressionable age of six, I was in awe of how she transformed my short, bitten nails into shiny "diamonds." From then on through grade school and high school, I continued to get manicures from her for every special event.

During my college years and after I was married, Golden continued to give me a manicure every week. She doted on me and over the years we became very close friends. I adored her. Listening to stories from her life were very special to me and we loved to laugh together.

I often confided in Golden and told her my dreams, as well as my disappointments.

One evening as she worked on my nails, I told her a story about an occasion that was humiliating for me when I first started working for the local bank. I had been employed for only three months before the annual Christmas dinner dance took place. My position as executive secretary to the bank president had placed me at the head table with him, his wife, and members of the board of directors, plus their spouses. Mostly because I was newly employed, I was very intimidated and nervous throughout the entire evening, but I maintained what I thought was a sophisticated composure. I managed to gracefully stand up and accept when the chairman of the board asked me to dance. Unfortunately, my composure ended when I tripped on the leg of a chair and almost fell to the floor. With good timing, the kind man managed to catch me before I fell, and with his polished dignity he acted as though nothing at all had happened. But, I was so embarrassed.

Fortunately, as we danced, we managed a pleasant conversation which helped me relax and forget the awkward moment. When the music ended, he turned to lead me back to my seat; however, we could not seem to back away from each other. I looked down to discover that the ribbon streamers from the satin belt on my evening dress had somehow wrapped around his belt buckle while we were dancing on the crowded floor.

We were the only ones left on the dance floor now and we were hooked together at the waist! As I glanced at the crowd, I saw many curious eyes on us. We tried to get our belts untangled, but as I pulled and tugged at my belt, my anxiety increased and so did the knots in the silky streamers. There was only one solution. We had to cut the streamers. Our next dilemma was how to manage to walk off the dance floor and find a pair of scissors. Being hooked at the waist did not allow us to walk side by side. Instead, we sort of did a side-step shuffle, face-to-face, off the dance floor. Looking for scissors to separate us, we ended up going through the lobby to the hotel's business office. What a sight we were and the strange looks we got from the people in the lobby confirmed it. Although I was mortified, the chairman of the board had a great sense of humor and when the ribbon streamers were finally cut we both nearly doubled over laughing from relief and from the absurdity of the situation.

As I told this story of my disastrous evening to Golden, I acted out the entire scene. I didn't think she was ever going to stop laughing. When she finally came up for air, she said, "RuthKay, you have a gift—the gift of making people laugh! Promise me as you go through life that you will share your gift with as many people as possible, for everyone needs to laugh."

That was over thirty years ago and I have never forgotten my blessed friend Golden or her advice. Today I share my gift of laughter with people who need to lighten up to become more successful and to improve their lives. I use humor in every program I present and it is very rewarding when I see people laughing and having fun.

Golden had a God-given gift of recognizing the talent I had and she lovingly encouraged me to make the best use of it.

Sometimes the conversations we have with our friends, family and confidants can help reveal things to us about ourselves that we may have overlooked. These conversations may also provide us with "words of wisdom" that can help us succeed in life. I listen carefully to friends, other speakers and experts, and I often write down their positive advice. Here are some examples:

Ann: "Do a little each day."
Sue: "Be consistent."
Karkles: "Don't look at the things you don't have. Look at the things you do have."
Tom: "Live in the moment."
Linda: "God loves you."
Mr. Brown: "Never look back."
Bobbi: "Go girl!"
Lisa: "Buy quality clothes and wear them to shreds."
Pam: "What's your point?"

Zig: "Act enthusiastic, and you will soon become enthusiastic!"

Rev. Ann: "Let's pray."

Shirley: "When you are down and out, count your blessings."

Mark: "Inside everyone is a genius."

Darrin: "Faith isn't faith until it's all you've got!"

Mrs. Bell: "I don't care what side of the tracks you come from. You are going to learn!"

Iyanla: "Don't give up five minutes before the miracle!"

Marilyn: "Think happy thoughts."

Take a few minutes to reflect and write down some of the encouraging messages you have heard from people whom you admire and respect. Refer to your list from time to time to stay inspired and motivated. Use your gifts!

Listen carefully to your mentors for sage advice.

*"Keep away from people
who try to belittle
your ambitions.
Small people always do that,
but the really great
make you feel that you, too,
can become great."*
—*Mark Twain*

✤ *11* ✤
Force Not!

After completing a sales training class for a large bank, I was scheduled to meet with the bank's president, the executive vice president and several senior officers to discuss the results of the training.

I arrived early for this appointment and the senior secretary ushered me into the meeting room for our conference, which just also happened to be the bank president's elegantly furnished private office. She told me that the president and his managers were in conference at the moment and they would all be there in about fifteen minutes to meet with me.

As I waited for the bank officers to arrive, I noticed that this beautiful room was not really set up appropriately for my presentation to them. I'm a professional speaker and I know the importance of having a room set up right whether it is for two people or for two thousand so I began rearranging the chairs. I soon discovered there were not enough seats for everyone. I found some big, plush, and cushy conference chairs in the adjoining room and I got right to work shuffling them into the president's office one by one.

Whew! It wasn't easy, but I was really on a roll and I had most of the huge chairs situated around the room in what I thought was a pleasing and workable arrangement. Now, only one more chair was needed to be pushed through the doorway to the president's office and then I would be ready for the meeting. This time, though, the door to his office was partly closed, so I pushed hard to open it and I felt a little resistance, as though a pillow or something soft was lodged behind it somehow. I was in a hurry! I didn't have time to check this situation out. The bank officers would be here soon and I was determined to finish my task before they arrived, so I shoved the door even harder, and as I rammed the big conference chair through the door opening, I thought I heard the "pillow" thing make a muffled grunting noise. Now, I know that pillows don't have sound effects and that doors don't make sounds like that either, so I cautiously peeked around the doorway and peered into the president's office.

The imposing and solemn president of the bank had apparently come into his office quietly and had been hanging up his coat in the closet next to the doorway, through which I had been hefting all this office furniture. The poor man was now ungainly stuffed face-first into his own coat closet with his hindquarters sticking out of the closet door. Needless to say, I was mortified and red-faced as I stammered a hasty apology to the once-dignified, but now-disheveled bank president. I was so embarrassed that I had forced open the door of his private office while the president was still behind it. Oh, why hadn't I just looked first?

I learned from this that in life when things are not working smoothly—don't force them. This lesson applies to not forcing something like a door that won't open, but it is also sound advice for not pushing things emotionally—like forcing the life back into a friendship or relationship that just doesn't work any longer.

Years ago I used to go to lunch every Friday with my friend Karen, whom I really admired. She seemed to be so good at everything—from decorating her house to working as a secretary for a lawyer. I had placed Karen on a pedestal and I wanted to be just like her. I entertained the thought of finding a secretarial position. Karen encouraged me to do so, and within a month I had found myself a job. Because of my enthusiasm and willingness to always go the "extra mile" for my employer, raises and promotions were soon offered to me. Whenever I had some good news about my job, I would share it with Karen during our Friday lunches. I thought she would be happy for me; however, I would inevitably end up feeling a little down-in-the-dumps. I couldn't quite figure out why our Friday lunches now made me feel drained and not very enthusiastic about going back to my office for the rest of the afternoon.

One Friday in mid-morning at work, my boss told me how pleased he was with my progress and ambitions and that he had decided to send me to a special two-day seminar for secretaries who wanted to enhance their professional skills and who desired further career training. When Karen and I met for lunch later I was elated about my news and I wanted to share it with her. She listened to me in stony silence, and then she sat up in her chair, slapped her hand on the restaurant table, and said in a firm voice, "RuthKay, I think you are just getting too carried away with your silly little job and you shouldn't put so much importance on it." After she'd said this, I had the same deflated feelings I'd had every other time we'd lunched together lately and I was at my wit's end.

It finally became apparent to me that the "little green monster" of envy was making Karen jealous of my progress at work because I was moving ahead faster in my job than she was in hers. She routinely made negative comments to me in order to downplay my successes. Even though I knew what was going on, I continued to go to lunch with Karen every Friday. To me, it was still very important to maintain this relationship because we had known each other for such a long time. I wanted to make the friendship work. Forcing it to stay alive, however, was not really healthy for me. Karen's toxic words and negativity had such an impact on me that I almost felt guilty about succeeding. I tried talking with Karen about this, but to no avail. It was heartbreaking for me to realize that Karen wasn't really a friend anymore and that she had no interest in changing her hurtful behavior. The friendship had outlived its usefulness.

At long last, I decided sadly that I would have to end our friendship. It took a tremendous amount of strength for me to do this, but after I did, I felt that a huge burden had been lifted. I was now free to be ambitious and successful. I also learned to cultivate warm and giving friendships that benefited me, as well as my friends. I knew then that I was well on the way to feeling better, to happily pursuing my goals, and to creating healthy and supportive relationships with true friends.

Face, don't force, negative situations or toxic relationships.

My Kodak® moment.

12

Hearts A' Pounding

My last banking job ended some years ago. I call myself a "recovering banker." One of my duties while working at the bank then was to assist our biggest commercial accounts with launching their new company products. On one particular occasion, I was coordinating an event sponsored at the bank by one of our largest bank customers.

They were giving a gala "open house" event to promote their new and expensive, fine line of vacation travel trailers. The Hollywood star, Patrick Duffy, known to millions as "Bobby Ewing" from the popular TV series Dallas, was invited to host the event. The first time I saw him on TV, I developed a huge crush on Patrick Duffy and I never missed an episode of Dallas.

The tickets were very exclusive and outrageously expensive and only the bank's senior officers could get tickets to attend this event. I begged the bank president to please, please find one of the highly sought after tickets for me so I could also go. After I whined for weeks and had fairly worn the bank president down to a frazzle, he finally gave in and said to me in his loud, gruff voice, "RuthKay, you're just like 'the squeaky wheel that gets the grease.' Here's your ticket. So, go! Just go!"

The big night finally arrived. Dressed in my navy blue suit, I looked like a distinguished and serious representative of the bank. I walked into the huge building where a group was viewing the film previews for Dallas. As I walked around the room networking with people, I turned the corner and I saw the most beautiful scenery I had ever seen. There he was . . . Patrick Duffy . . . plus lots of women. They were lined up to get a hug and have their photo taken with the star. I got in line, too, feeling like a giddy teen-ager, eagerly awaiting my turn. My heart started pounding as I stepped forward into the light of this charming hunk of a man. My handsome hero smiled at me and said, "Well, hello there!" and he gave me a wonderful and massive bear hug. As the photographer captured this occurrence on film, I practically melted in my shoes.

My knees felt weak and I definitely had stars in my eyes after being enveloped in Patrick's wonderful embrace as I continued to walk around the room to do more networking. Like a moth to a flame, I kept finding myself gravitating back toward the same corner to see "Bobby" just one more time . . . and that's when the thought jumped into my head . . . "What would be wrong if I got in line for another big hug and a another photo?" I mused. Just one more chance to look at that gorgeous face and those dreamy eyes. "Why, he has hugged hundreds of women tonight and he'd never remember me!" I thought. So with my heart pounding, I got back in line again. When it was my turn to be in the star's blinding presence, he said to me, "Well, hi, sweetheart. I see you're back again." I couldn't help but giggle and blush like a kid when he obviously had remembered me out of all the women he'd held in his arms that evening. Then he gave me another one of his huge, wonderful hugs, smiled his charming "Bobby Ewing" Texas smile, and winked at me. It was one of life's sweetest joys . . . and what a great memory to relive once more whenever I need a lift.

Relive your past joys.

*"Every problem
contains a gift."*
—Richard Bach

❧ 13 ❧
A Broken Spirit

I asked my mother for an increase in my allowance when I was 12 years old. Unfortunately, Mother did not agree to it. I sulked and pouted about it and felt that the increase was justified because, goodness knows, I had things to buy! Getting nowhere with changing my mother's mind, my desire for more money forced me to think of a creative way to earn it.

I decided to give baton twirling lessons to the younger girls in my neighborhood and I charged 50 cents an hour. Twirling had been a practiced activity of mine from the time I was seven years old and I knew that I could teach the girls what I had already learned. At the age of 12 though, I did not realize what an impact teaching the art of baton twirling would have on my entire life.

By the time I was 17, I had opened up my own studio and named it *The R.K. Baton Twirling Studio.* I had three twirling corps: the RUTHETTES, the KAYETTES, and the SPEARETTES were my senior corps. I called my 3 and 4-year-old twirlers, "RuthKay's Little Bunnies." We traveled throughout the country to participate in parades and competitions. My students' parents accompanied us on our many trips and they were very helpful.

My twirling business, which began from a disgruntled 12-year old's desire for more money than her allowance, grew into a successful venture that allowed me to buy a car, clothes, plus pay for college.

After I was married, I continued to live, breathe and dream twirling. I was either teaching, traveling, or making plans for the next event, which caused conflicts in my marriage. Finally, I had to give up the twirling business. I felt like my spirit had been broken and I went into a deep depression.

Many people couldn't understand why I became so depressed from that experience and it was even difficult for me to understand it, too. With the help of several knowledgeable counselors, I discovered that since I had been emotionally, physically and sexually abused as a child, my twirling had become an escape for me. Whether I was teaching young girls to become baton twirling champions or whether I was performing a twirling routine myself in front of an audience, it made me feel special and worthy. I did not have to deal with the pain I'd felt as a child, because twirling became my entire existence. It was the salve on my serious wounds. Without that medicinal protection, however, I became very depressed.

Being cognizant of the origin of my depression did not ease it though. The depression lasted for several years. I prayed every day for God to help me overcome my depression. And one day my prayers were answered. It became crystal clear to me—I needed to show initiative and take action rather than waiting for something to happen. God helped me understand that I must take the first step toward recovering and He would guide me. In God's infinite wisdom, He knew what would help heal my heart and spirit. Little did I know at that time that my career as a motivational speaker would develop from my quest to overcome depression.

My enthusiasm and energy began to grow as I made plans to go back to college. But that was not enough to help me regain my self-esteem. I had to find additional activities that were challenging and rewarding. Therefore, I took on small jobs as well.

Initially I worked as a file clerk for an insurance agency, then as an errand person for a law firm. Finally, I took on a greater responsibility as a legal secretary, and later as an executive secretary for a bank president. A promotion as the bank's marketing representative introduced me to audiotapes by Zig Ziglar, a world renowned motivational speaker. I loved his enthusiasm, philosophy and humor. Listening to his tapes and attending his seminars gave me the courage to prepare to become a motivational speaker. Since 1983, I have been successfully motivating and helping people become the best they can be. And in the process I have overcome my feelings of despair and anxiety.

As I look back over the experience that forced me to change the direction of my life, I see a positive outcome in the seemingly negative dilemma. Life has a way of coming full circle. Recently, a former baton twirling student of mine, now in a top management position in her company, hired me to do a motivational program for her employees. As I finished making the arrangements with her, I hung up the phone and chuckled, "Life couldn't get any better than this!"

A broken spirit doesn't have to mean a broken life.

🦋 *14* 🦋
Mending Hearts

My friend Shirley told me one evening on the phone that we should treat all people as if they have a broken heart. I didn't get the full meaning of that until much later when I presented a program at an investment company about using laughter and music as a diversion from stress and pain.

Everyone in the audience seemed to enjoy themselves that day throughout the three-hour program except for one solemn-faced lady in the back row. She seemed detached and not really part of the group, and she seldom let even a hint of a smile cross her face. She was really distracting my attention and I immediately judged her as having a "bad attitude." At the end of the program, as people lined up to shake hands with me and comment on the enjoyable presentation, this woman walked hesitantly toward me.

I admit that the "bad attitude" I'd perceived coming from her had made me feel defensive and also a little nervous and unsettled. I like people to be entertained and have fun during my programs, as much as I enjoy giving them a good learning experience. Since I felt that this lady's detachment and somberness was related to something I'd said . . . something, perhaps, she didn't like . . . I have to admit that I found myself to be sort of irritated at her. But to my surprise, this quiet woman greeted me with a smile and leaned forward to say in a soft voice, "RuthKay, I thoroughly enjoyed your presentation."

Butterfly wings could have knocked me over, and I couldn't help but show my genuine surprise. "I'm sorry if it appeared that I didn't like your program," she continued almost in a whisper. "You see, my husband died three days ago. We bury him tomorrow. I want you to know that for three hours, you kept me entertained and you distracted me from my pain. That has gone a long way toward getting me through today, and will help me get through the funeral tomorrow. Thank you for letting me forget my sorrow for a little while. You have also given me hope—hope for the future, and that my days are not going to always be grim. I will never forget you." We wrapped our arms around each other. She pulled back from me with a beaming smile and tears streaming down her face. We cried and laughed and cried again, as though we were old friends now.

As I thought about this bereaved woman later, my friend Shirley's words echoed in my head: "Treat all people as though they have a broken heart." A broken heart can be hidden and we need to be aware that what people show on the outside may be very different from what is really going on within. It also means there's no appropriate time for harsh judgments—or any judgments at all.

Put judgments and criticism aside.

"WOW! Just for me? I love surprises!"

🦋 *15* 🦋
The Power of Little Things

I have made it a habit to notice and become excited about the little things that happen to me on a daily basis. For example, one evening before giving a keynote presentation in Chicago, I arrived early for dinner at the hotel restaurant. The waiter politely told me that I was the restaurant's first customer that evening and that they weren't open for business yet, so would I mind waiting in the lounge for about 20 minutes?

"The first customer!" I said to him. "Wow! Does this mean I get a prize?" I asked with a big smile on my face.

"Well, I'll see what I can do," snickered the waiter as he led me to a white covered table in the hotel lounge. To my surprise, he returned a few minutes later bearing a dessert cart that he wheeled smartly up in front of my table. He stood back, whipped off the cover from a large silver platter on the cart and then made a wide bow as he presented before me the biggest, the fattest, chocolate-covered strawberry I had ever seen. It looked like it had just been picked from the farm. It was so fresh looking with its perky green cap of leaves—the shiny redness under it showing it had ripened to perfection. The sheen of the chocolate surrounding it completed this most wonderful strawberry—and it was just for me!

I felt like a small child at Christmas, and I squealed and clapped my hands with delight!

The waiter said he'd never seen anyone become so excited about a strawberry. After all, it was such a "little thing." "Yes, I guess it is," I replied. "But, you know, that's really what life is all about, isn't it? I mean, celebrating the 'little' things."

Small pleasures will be more abundant in our lives than grandiose ones, so we need to celebrate even the tiniest events and mark their occurrences with our gratitude and delight. For example, right now give yourself a standing ovation for all your achievements, big and small. Yes, you may develop a few laugh lines, but they will be worth the effort!

Get excited about the little things to gain a new appreciation for life!

🦋 *16* 🦋
Bouncing Bellies

Whatever you do, put everything you've got into it. This bit of knowledge came to me at an early age. It occurred to me that this philosophy also applied to yawning. In my experience as a professional speaker, I have discovered there are actually two kinds of yawns. First, the "Grand Canyon" yawn is when you open up your mouth so wide your lips curl back, almost making a circle around your entire face—you know, a hole so big you could throw a basketball into it! The other kind of yawn is when you try to be very polite and not let anyone actually see you yawn. This is done by lowering your head and then sucking your whole face to the back of your neck by inhaling a great gulp of air. This "polite" yawn sooner or later creates hundreds of horizontal wrinkles from the chin on down to the bottom of your neck. So you might as well make it a big yawn, and save yourself a few lines in the process. As I am demonstrating the "Grand Canyon" yawn, I encourage people to really yawn with everything they've got and to enjoy it.

The same philosophy applies to laughing. Laugh with everything you've got and laugh out loud, too. Chances are when you are laughing, your belly is going to bounce a bit. Watch it bounce, and it will make you laugh even more. Now, if you don't have a belly, look around and watch someone else's bounce.

My friend Stacey has a shy, seven-year-old boy named Jimmy. When Jimmy laughs, he closes his mouth and keeps his head very stiff, holding in his laugh while his head jerks back and forth. When I catch him doing this, I always slap him on the back and say, "Jimmy, open your mouth and laugh with your whole body. If you don't, your laugh will get stuck in there and won't be able to find its way out! And besides, Jimmy, laughter is good for you."

Some time ago, my son, Darrin, was having chest pains and had to be hospitalized. Since I knew that laughter can serve as a distraction from pain, I would call him every day and we would exchange funny stories and jokes over the phone. Darrin has a fantastic sense of humor and he laughs from the top of his head right on down to his toes. It seems to go right through his entire body. In fact, the nurses said they could hear him laughing all over the hospital and they said they weren't sure if he really needed to be in there at all. Our fun, daily phone visits were very comforting to me because I knew that when Darrin was laughing, he was also healing. Laughing literally does your heart good.

It is my belief that we all have an "inner giggle"— a childlike love of finding delight in being happy. And if you have a habit of suppressing your laughter, why not let your "inner giggle" wiggle and jiggle a little? As Norman Cousins, author of *Anatomy of an Illness* said, "Laughter is a form of internal jogging. Laughter helps revitalize and reenergize your entire body, which in turn, helps you fight against potential illnesses." If you already have a few wrinkles, a big belly laugh will help keep those face lines from drooping.

Let go and laugh with your entire body.

"If someone makes me laugh, I'm her slave for life."
—Bette Midler

🦋 *17* 🦋
Where's the Glue?

I awoke the morning of an important presentation I would make later that day and began the process of getting myself ready for it. First, I walked down the hall and was greeted with the round, brown evidence of my pet's accident on the living room rug. My little dog, Benji, sat on the floor next to his dirty deed with a bewildered look on his face and looked up at me as if to say, "Well, don't blame me! I don't know how that got there!"

Next, my search for the morning newspaper led me to find it on the roof of the house. Oh, that newspaper boy! I guess I could forget reading the funnies that day, I thought. And, then I discovered that the blue suit I'd planned to wear for my presentation that afternoon had been jammed at the back of my closet and was full of wrinkles.

Actually, the wrinkles didn't bother me very much because I had an idea for a solution to this problem. I'd heard that if you hang a garment over the tub in the bathroom on the shower curtain rod and turn on the hot water in the shower full force, that after about twenty minutes the steam would make the wrinkles magically disappear. So, I set out to do just that.

Alas, one of my kids must have messed with the shower lever because when I leaned over the tub and turned on the faucet, the water from the shower head cascaded down onto my perfect hairdo. There I stood gasping in front of the tub, water dripping down my hair and make-up. I now resembled a sheep dog caught in a rainstorm. "Okay! Let's get a positive attitude about this!" I said to myself later in the mirror as I repaired my drowned hairdo.

Back again to the bathroom I went to check on my suit and see if the wrinkles in it had all disappeared. Oh, no! I just about got sick to my stomach when I saw my beautiful blue wool suit floating in the tub of steaming hot water. The plastic hanger had broken in half from the weight of the suit causing it to fall into the tub, and of course, the drain was closed, so the tub was rapidly filling with hot water.

I took several deep breaths now, hoping that would help keep myself "glued" together. Back to the bedroom I went to search the closet for another suit to wear. "What next?" I thought. This was really an incredibly frustrating morning and it was only 9 o'clock! I gathered all my materials together for my afternoon presentation and went into the garage where I began loading them into the car. Just then I heard a hissing sound—like I was losing air in one of my car tires. Sssssssssss. This really put me into a frantic mode. "Oh, no, all I need now is a flat tire!" I thought as I slammed the box of materials onto the garage floor.

I ran around the car checking each tire and I couldn't find a leak in any one of them, but still the faint "Sssssssssss" sound persisted. "Where is that coming from?" I asked. I listened again. "Ssssssss." The noise seemed to be coming from inside the car. I opened the door to the back seat and heard it clearer now, "Sssssssss." There on the floor of the back seat was a six-pack of Coca-Cola® making the ominous hissing noise. One of the Coke® cans had an itsy bitsy little hole in it and it was slowly spewing a sticky brown sweet mist over the entire back seat of my car. "Oh no! No!" I groaned. My positive attitude was leaving faster than that leaky can of soda.

That's when the "glue" holding me together that morning started to lose its strength and I could just feel myself start to "unravel." I went back into the house and through to the kitchen, where I stood and stared at the phone. "I just don't believe this is all happening to me! I should have stayed in bed this morning." I moaned.

I know turning to a good friend can help in a stressful time like this, and I really felt like I could use a some friendly help. Thank heavens my presentation was scheduled for the late afternoon so that meant I had plenty of time to "get it all glued together" again before then. I decided to call the most positive and enthusiastic person I knew, my pal Suzie, and tell her of my exasperating woes. When Suzie answered the phone, she sounded upbeat and perky as usual and also glad to hear from me. What a treasure she was. Suzie listened as I related my unbelievable "whine" list and she was so supportive and understanding. "RuthKay," she said, "let's go have a nice lunch, have some laughs, and see if we can turn the rest of your day around." Oh, that sounded like a great plan to me.

A burst of sunshine named Suzie greeted me when I walked into the restaurant. Suzie settled comfortably into her chair at our favorite table knowing that I had the awful events of the day to rant and rave about. Her comments were light, gentle, and funny and I soon began to latch onto her positive energy. Slowly I started to see the hilarity and humor in my foibles. We filled our lunch time together with laughter at all the unbelievable bits of bad luck I'd had that day and all of a sudden I didn't feel like such a victim anymore.

Afterward Suzie went back to her office and I went on to give one of the best presentations I'd ever done. I felt absolutely wonderful now. I had regained my composure from the morning's events and now looked at them as nothing more than a string of totally unexpected bumps in my road of life. I felt reenergized by the TLC and positive, caring attitude of a good friend who helped me turn a disastrous day into a delightful one.

When your world is falling apart, caring, understanding, and enthusiastic friends can help glue it back together again.

"One size doesn't fit all!"

❦ 18 ❦
I'd Rather Have a Root Canal!

When conducting workshops for women, I first ask them if they think they are strong and if they can survive life's struggles. They confidently exclaim, "Yes! Yes! Yes!" and their enthusiasm escalates. Then I shout, "Of course we can survive the struggles" ... as I pull a pair of pantyhose out of my briefcase ... "because we have to get into THESE every day." They nearly roll over laughing.

Personally, I find it a real effort in the morning just getting ready for work. First I look at the pair of pantyhose that I just took out of the package, and then I look in the mirror at my body, which is shaped like a gargantuan pear. It's not easy for me to get into these little nylon "leg jackets." I have to talk to myself and it's usually negative. I loudly proclaim, "I'd rather have a root canal!" And then the struggle begins.

What a sight this is! My legs and arms are going in opposite directions. I begin to sweat; my face turns red; and my veins pop out. My backside and hips start moving in a sort of "mambo" motion while I simultaneously jump up and down, hoping the sheer force of gravity will aid my body in the final entry to get the pantyhose over my hips and up to my waist and smooth out all places in between. If someone were to video tape me putting on my pantyhose and submit it to the TV show, America's Funniest Home Videos, I know I'd probably win the Grand Prize. I huff and puff as if I'm doing a high-impact work-out.

One day, my daughter, who was ten years old at the time, had a friend staying over. Her friend asked about all the noise coming from my bedroom. She said it sounded like a three thousand pound elephant or hippo from the zoo doing an aerobic exercise. My daughter laughed and laughed. "It's just my mother putting on her pantyhose," she told her friend.

Although I disliked wearing pantyhose, I discovered that they definitely solved a problem that could have gotten in the way of my career advancement. When I worked in a bank and was moving up the ranks, my mentor told me it was important to project a positive, professional and powerful image through my body language. She said I needed to stand and sit up straight. Though I tried hard to follow her advice, I would find myself slumping at the board meetings I attended, especially when I was tired or under a lot of stress. My shoulders would move slightly forward and down, setting off a chain reaction. As my lower back curled up in response to my sagging shoulders my belly would rise and my boobs would drop down, causing them both to meet in the middle. Instead of looking like a sharp, powerful corporate executive, I looked like a rumpled bag of laundry.

To counteract this unprofessional image, I would wear my TALL, super-duper, control top pantyhose that stretched over the lumps and bumps of my midriff. These pantyhose may have been a bit longer in the leg, but they were so tight that I felt like an Egyptian mummy wearing a giant rubber band wrapped around my mid-section. The minute I would slouch or bend over, the pressure from the elastic waistband of the super-duper-taller-but-leaner pantyhose would start to cut off my breathing and would force me to stand up straight. After wearing these pantyhose for several months, I finally solved my slouching problem and I was able to project professionalism like my mentor had advised. Even though I still hate getting into my pantyhose I have finally learned to get them on by using patience and also the help of upbeat music.

I get lots of e-mails and notes from women thanking me for my seminars. Many of them say, "Every time I put on my pantyhose, I remember you and I start laughing!" Their comments often make me smile and I always appreciate hearing from them. I want to be known as a person who helps people laugh their socks (whoops! I mean, pantyhose) off.

We can survive the struggles.

❦ *19* ❦
Hokey Stuff

This is a question I always ask my audiences: "How many of you have been under stress lately?" It never fails—usually 85% to 90% agree that they are constantly under stress. And I ask, just how do they deal with stress? Many respond by telling me they eat chocolate, have sex, go shopping, exercise, take a bubble bath, or read a good book, etc.

"Oh, that's great," I affirm, nodding my head. Then, I share with them how I cope with stress. I tell them that I'm a runner and I demonstrate by running from one end of the stage to the other. This usually gets a few chuckles and lots of raised eyebrows as I see them all mentally imagining me decked out in running gear with a sweatband around my little pointed head. "Yes! I am a runner!" I persist. "Why, when I am under stress I run back-and-forth to the refrigerator just as fast as I can!" And, I go on to tell them that if I don't stop running to the refrigerator that one of these days I will probably become my own zip code.

I am also known for wearing two differently colored shoes for my programs . . . Yes! on purpose. But it didn't start out that way. I will never forget the morning I got ready to speak to a group of 2,000 sales people brought together for their annual convention at one of the country's most fashionable resort hotels. The sales reps attending this convention were *la creme de la creme* of their companies and were known for being smartly dressed, as well as successful.

So, I was more than a little preoccupied with facing that many influential business people, and in my haste at dressing that morning I had put on one red shoe and one black shoe ... without realizing it. I rushed to grab one of the last available taxis and sped on towards the convention center at the edge of the resort where I would give my presentation. When I arrived and started mingling with the crowd, I noticed that people would look at my shoes and then glance up at my face. Some looked and snickered; some laughed outright; some just smiled and glanced away; and some looked at me quizzically and downright disgusted. Finally, I had to look down at my shoes, too. Then I understood why they were laughing.

Oh, no! I wanted to just sink into the floor and disappear. What could I do? I couldn't go back to my room because I had traveled 30 miles from the resort hotel to the convention center. And all I had with me were my purse and briefcase, and neither one contained a spare pair of shoes. I felt trapped and so self-conscious! I was forced to wear the mismatched shoes all day.

Now, I am a firm believer that things happen for a reason, and although I was embarrassed by this blunder, I knew I had to think quickly to try to turn this situation around. Since most people were amused by my odd pair of shoes they probably thought I had made this fashion gaffe on purpose. I decided to flaunt my mistake, and I laughed along with the crowd.

Because I was extremely nervous prior to this particular presentation, the "shoe goof" distracted me from my nervousness and gave me a chance to pull myself together to relax so I could successfully connect with my audience.

Remember, laughter distracts you from stress. When you have to deal with "icky-picky" annoyances at work—like those days when the coffee machine blows up, the fax machine jams, your computer won't boot up, or you can't log on to the Internet because of a traffic jam in cyberspace—try to find a "funny" in it and it will help to distract you from the hassles.

And how about that psychic copy machine? My theory is that copy machines are like elephants. They are huge and gray and also have long-term memories—they never forget! They always get even with you for every bad thing you have ever said about or done to them! When I first walk into my office in the morning, I always greet my copy machine with a cheerful, "Good morning. My, you look good in gray." Then, I give the copier a big hug and say, "We have a lot of work to do today, and I know you will cooperate and do a great job!" Then I press the warm-up button, and I encourage my copier with a cheer, "Okay, now gimmee a 'C,' gimmee an 'O,' gimmee a 'P,' gimmee a 'Y!' Rah! Rah! Rah! COPY!" and I jump in the air and clap my hands.

And as you visualize this comic dialogue with your office equipment, you will likely be distracted from your morning stress. Try this any time of the day, and you just might start laughing. You are probably thinking this is pretty "hokey" office behavior and you simply would never act this way, at least not at eight o'clock in the morning!

However, I invite you to just THINK about doing it.

Sometimes it's "okey-dokey" to be "hokey." Being, acting and just thinking silly is a great stress reliever. When you are faced with those irksome, annoying little "happenstances" at work, or while driving, or at home, slow down and take a laugh break . . . even if it's only for a minute. Allow yourself to be a little bit "hokey!" You will see that laughter DISTRACTS you easily from your stress, and allows you to gain control over these annoying inconveniences.

Let laughter take the "icky" out of the "picky" little annoyances.

*"Imagination is more
important
than knowledge."
—Albert Einstein*

❦ 20 ❦

Spots and No Shoulder Pads

Before leaving on a trip to Florida, I stopped at the dry cleaners, then hurriedly packed the newly cleaned clothes into my suitcase, and dashed to the airport. The next day in Miami as I was getting ready for an important meeting, I pulled my suit jacket out of the cleaner's plastic bag and noticed that "the spot" they were supposed to have removed was still there. And the cleaners also forgot to put the shoulder pads back in. I panicked and scrunched up my face in fury (from which I'm sure I contracted several new frown lines). Since I am shaped like a pear, I desperately needed my shoulder pads to balance out my figure. They make me appear taller and slimmer and I've gotten so used to wearing them with just about everything—even T-shirts. With every minute that ticked away, my frustration grew. It was one hour before the meeting, and I had brought only the one suit. What was I going to do?

After my initial fit of anger, I gathered my composure, went out on my hotel balcony and took some deep breaths of the balmy Florida air. I sat down, closed my eyes, and tuned out the world so I could tap into my creative imagination. How could I solve my problem?

It worked! I had an idea. I ran into the bathroom where I borrowed two washcloths from the hotel and pinned one to each shoulder area to substitute for the missing shoulder pads. They looked even better than the original pads in my jacket. My butterfly pin that I always wear was exactly the right size to cover the offending spot, and thank Heavens, the spot was in just the right place where the butterfly pin should go. A dash of creativity goes a long way when problem solving in our daily lives.

Many years ago I had a boring job as a file clerk for an insurance company. Every day I had to file millions of documents—well, it seemed like millions—and for six hours a day. The job was really getting to me. All I could think about was filing. It even crept into my dreams and my dreams became boring too. As the filing seemed to take over my life, the wrinkles and crinkles rapidly appeared, and I knew I had to do something fast just to keep my sanity. Maybe I needed to tap into my childlike creativity. I remember many times when that creativity saved the day for me. For example, as a kid, I spent many long hours by myself and had to use my creativity to keep myself entertained. I had an imagination that would have impressed Einstein. You wouldn't believe the excuses I came up with for getting a bad grade in geography. Then as a teenager, I created over a hundred reasons for coming home late from a date. My childhood creativity rescued me before and it might help me as an adult to cope with my boring job.

I took time to find a quiet place in my mind where the wondrous child with the vivid imagination still lives. This sparked a wonderful idea—I decided I would make a game of this tedious job. I would have contests with myself every day to see how many pieces of paper I could accurately and swiftly file, and every day I would set out to break my own record. When I did break a daily record, I would celebrate by buying something special for myself—big or small, like an ice cream cone, a trinket for the house, or something pretty to wear. Soon I started to love my job and the little game I had created. I developed a newfound enthusiasm for my work. Management noticed my positive attitude, too, and the energy I was putting into my job. Before long, I was offered a promotion.

Now, when I am trying to come up with ideas for my business or to resolve sticky problems, I've found that if I allow myself to go within and think as a curious child would, I can tap into my creativity. I am convinced we are all born with this productive talent—it just has to be developed. Watching children at play gives credence to that. Their active imaginations make anything possible for them to believe. Children are always living "in the moment" and they create their own exciting world. Keep your mind on "living in the now" and work at developing an inventive thought process that will help you solve problems by thinking more intuitively. It's a lot more fun than just staring at the clock hands pushing on towards five!

If there are obstacles and roadblocks along the path to attaining your goals, do these things: go to a quiet place, be still, relax, take a few deep breaths, and become like an inquisitive child again. Let your imagination soar and believe that anything is possible. You will be surprised by the creative ideas that may come to you.

Use child-like creative thinking to help find solutions to the dilemmas of life.

🦋 *21* 🦋

Do You Have Gas?

I was on my way to visit a prospective client one afternoon and since I was relatively new to the big city, I quickly became lost in the maze of traffic and streets that had a lot of similar names. This is not unusual for me. I can even get lost with a hand-drawn map and the best of directions, but the minute I think I'm lost I immediately take action! I pulled into one of those twenty-four hour convenience stores that sell everything from baby diapers to gasoline.

Into the store I went with high hopes of getting some good directions when I realized that I had walked in on an argument between the shift manager and one of his clerks who worked behind the counter. The clerk had apparently made a big mistake when totaling up a gasoline sale with other purchases a customer had just made. While the manager rudely barked at his employee, he was also staring right at me as he scowled and snarled. Something flashed into my mind that I remembered Zig Ziglar saying about a similar kind of tyrant, "He's the kind of guy who could brighten up a whole room just by leaving it." I felt a little uneasy, but I stepped up to the counter to ask for directions. But before I could even get my mouth open, the manager asked me in a loud, bullying voice, "Do you have gas?" After I recovered from my shock by the behavior of this rude gorilla, I just smiled at him, held my hand over my stomach and replied, "No, not today, but I did last weekend! I went on a picnic, ate baked beans and fried chicken, and it was a 'windy' day!"

The manager was just like a frozen rope—he never moved a muscle. Then all of a sudden, he let out a belly laugh you could hear all over the city. He was no longer the grouchy monster I had dreaded to ask for directions.

I learned an important lesson that day. First, when you are confronted with an uncomfortable situation, stand back a little and look for the "funny" in it—you know, kind of like a comedian would do on stage when faced with an annoying heckler. This will not only get you laughing, but it also might save face for you and for others. This way, YOU take charge of the situation by diffusing someone's anger.

Every time you let minor irritations upset you, it can take the sunshine out of what could have been a beautiful day. Instead, take to heart the advice given in the title of Richard Carlson's book, *Don't Sweat The Small Stuff . . . and It's All Small Stuff.* We must remember that it's often the "small stuff" that causes wrinkles. You can make a fun difference in another person's day.

Look for the "funny" in everyday events.

22

The Great Escape

After hundreds of years of marriage, my husband and I divorced. Although we had many problems in our marriage, there were also many good times, too. For one thing, he was an excellent cook, and I especially miss the evening meals he used to prepare for us. You see, I have always been challenged in the area of cuisine and culinary skills. My kitchen where I now live has two cleverly designed signs hanging on the wall. When you walk into my kitchen the first sign says: "The only reason I have a kitchen at all is because it came with the house." Over the stove I have another sign that says: "My next house won't have a kitchen—just vending machines!" This gives my guests plenty of warning not to expect too much from my kitchen and me.

Newly-divorced, one evening when I was trying to choke down a leftover I couldn't identify, I turned on the TV for a little company to go along with my meal, and the show "The Golden Girls" was on. I soon became caught up in their zany escapades and found I was laughing out loud and having a terrific evening all by myself. Enjoying the funny sitcom and laughing helped me escape into their wacky world for a little while which then helped me to forget my loneliness.

That particular comedy program lightened up what I thought was otherwise going to be a drab evening alone with my dinner in front of the TV. It was just one of many shows that really helped me survive the aftermath of my divorce and the daily stresses I encountered then as a newly-single person. After that, I regularly added humorous TV programs to my nightly dinner menu.

If you are trying to survive a divorce, some misfortune, or other rough times in your life, I encourage you to escape by watching funny videos and TV sitcoms, listening to humorous audio tapes, and to collect light reading material that will help you really let go and laugh.

Believe me, laughter will certainly ease your adjustment to the painful changes that may come your way throughout your life!

Painful changes become more manageable with laughter.

❧ *23* ❧
Whining & Wailing!

One fine spring morning I had just sat down to read the newspaper when I heard a loud "thud" behind me. I whipped around in my chair to look and I could tell by the feathers floating lazily down past my picture window that another bird had miscalculated her flight pattern and had hit the clear glass. I looked outside and sure enough the poor little thing was lying motionless on my porch.

This is what happens to some of us when we are faced with difficult changes in our lives—we hit our own glass wall when we are unable to cope. Just like the little bird, we can be completely stunned until we can get on our feet again. Human beings naturally resist making changes. Change can be scary. We like to stay safe with what we know and our comfort zone lies there inside the status quo.

Personally, I know very well how difficult it is to accept change. In fact, you could say that I am the "poster girl" for fighting change of any kind. I have resisted making changes all my life. It doesn't really matter what kind of change it is, whether it is learning a new computer program, having to take a detour on the highway, or even something as simple as changing a hairstyle. For example, I informed my hair stylist years ago that whenever we talk about me trying a new style, it makes me so nervous that we both might have to be sedated so we can get through the ordeal of adjusting to a new "hairdo." Simply put, I just don't like change!

In high school I was confronted with having to update some of my baton-twirling routines that I had laboriously perfected. I was the head baton twirler on my squad and I did solo performances during halftime at the football games. Doing the same old routines game after game was a piece of cake for me and very comfortable because there wasn't much of a chance that I would make a mistake. After all, I could do those old routines in my sleep.

One afternoon as I was practicing, my twirling coach said, "RuthKay, if you are going to continue to be the head twirler, you can't keep doing the same old routines. We've got to have something new." Because of my aversion to change, I was absolutely furious with my coach's comments and I began to whine and wail. "Well, what's wrong with what I've been doing? I don't want to learn a whole new routine!" I whined. I will have to admit that deep down inside I was getting bored with some of the old routines I performed at every game, but I resisted having to revise things because everything was going so well. I was afraid to take a chance because I might make some major goofs during a performance and the crowd might laugh at me. My coach was asking me to step outside the comfort zone I had created for myself. But against my will, I added new twirls to my routine, all the while continuing to feel sorry for myself. I'd hit the "glass wall" and I had to get up and learn how to "fly" again.

Over the years I have discovered that continuous complaining and resisting change has not only caused me stress, it has also caused stress for everyone around me.

Complaining is just like spraying yourself with insect repellent . . . it not only keeps the bugs away, but also the people. When we are faced with restructuring something that impacts our careers, or our personal lives, we need to give ourselves permission to express the fear, frustration, or sadness that may result from that change.

Expressing these emotions is a healthy response; however, the key to really successfully coping with change is to put a time line on the whining and the wailing. If you don't, you'll get stuck in the muck of fear and resentment and never progress. We get comfortable with just whining. It sort of postpones the inevitable. And change is inevitable! It has to come in order for us to grow and learn. If we don't make changes willingly, life usually has a nasty way of doing it for us. It's better to be able to make our own decisions to move forward in life rather than having to deal with things that will certainly be thrust upon us if we don't. As the old saying goes, "Nothing is as certain as change."

I was invited to present my workshop on *The Power of Laughter in a Changing Workplace* to the female executives of a large corporation that was undergoing a merger and a complete reorganization from the top level down. These corporate women had a collection of complaints about how their worlds, both corporate and personal, had been impacted by these changes. Some were fearful and uncertain about their futures, some were angry and resentful that they had not been part of the decision-making process and some were depressed, detached and feeling powerless. As part of a group "therapy" kind of session, I passed around Dr. Klucko (my rubber chicken) to help these women executives laugh, vent, talk, and to just "get it all out."

Since these women executives were angry and frustrated about the numerous changes taking place within their company, I encouraged them to voice their complaints to Dr. Klucko by either slamming the Doc on the conference table or stomping on him as they shouted out their frustrations. At first they balked at this, thinking it was undignified or silly, but soon they were all participating and they ended up laughing hysterically at themselves.

Just from observing these high-powered and highly-stressed women voice their fears about change and resolve to get themselves moving again, I knew they were going to be successful with all the new developments within their company. After that exercise, there was a big difference in their behavior. When the laughter died down, they all seemed to be relaxed and relieved. There were a number of reasons why this exercise was so effective. First, they all had an opportunity to vent their fear and anger in a safe environment. Second, the entire group participated. Third, they were very supportive of each other because they knew they were all in this merger together and had to act as a group to accept the scary changes. And, lastly and most importantly, they were given an opportunity to laugh together, and that took a lot of their fear away.

When you feel engulfed with stressful changes, I encourage you to let go and vent in a safe environment with people you trust. When you hit that "glass wall" of change, it is comforting to have a friend listen to you rant and rave a little and to help you let it all out. Then you'll be able to fly again! Once you have put a voice to your fears and resentments about having to make those life adjustments, then you need to get going.

Get your action plan in motion, and you will get out of the immobilizing fear of change. Get up and fly again!

Put a timeline on the whining and wailing. Go forward with courage to make the changes that confront you!

*"Wrinkles merely indicate
where the
smiles have been."*
—Mark Twain

🦋 24 🦋
Wrinkles At Their Best

My popularity always drops a notch when I tell a group of women that smiling is a "wrinkle-maker." I can immediately see their faces respond and the smiles fade around the room as they try to remain expressionless . . . and "wrinkle-less." But, they all seem to relax when I go on to explain that although smiling may cause a few wrinkles, it's still an instant beautifier and it enhances the quality of their lives, as well as enriches the lives of those on the receiving end of their wonderful smiles.

I not only discovered early in my life the benefits of smiling, but I also became familiar with the negative outcomes of *not* smiling. I entered my first baton twirling contest at the age of eight, determined to win first place. But, to my surprise, I didn't win a thing.

So up I walked to the judge's table and with one hand perched on my hip, I looked her square in the eye and asked, "Judge, just why didn't I win?" I was a spunky little kid!

The judge responded seriously by telling me that it was because I didn't smile at all while I was performing. She explained that a major part of my score was based on personality projection, which included smiling.

I remembered those words when I practiced getting ready to enter my second contest. I marched out that day and did my routine using my "industrial-strength" smile, grinning from ear to ear, but I still didn't win. In response to my indignant question of "How come I didn't win this time?" the judge told me my smile looked frozen and that I needed to smile more "naturally." These instructions left me completely frustrated. I thought a smile was a smile, and now I had to learn to do it "naturally?"

To solve this "smile problem," my mother took me to Miss DePaul, a former Las Vegas showgirl. She was vivacious and full of enthusiasm and had a fabulous smile. This woman taught me how to smile effortlessly and how to project my personality to the judges and the audience while I was twirling. I put everything Miss DePaul taught me into practice and fearlessly entered my third contest. This time I won! What a thrill! I didn't realize at the time just how much that smiling would impact my entire life.

A smile is a universal welcome that has many benefits. It brightens up your whole face, it helps you really connect with people, it gives your face "life" . . . and it's an inexpensive way to instantly improve on your looks.

A smile also touches your heart when you are hurting. A number of years ago when my mother was dying of cancer, I came to her bedside to say good-bye. She had been in a coma for several days and I was so afraid in her frail state she wouldn't know I was there or she wouldn't be able to acknowledge my presence. As I walked into the hospital room, her nurse told her, "RuthKay is here." Amazingly, mother awoke from her deep state of unconsciousness and slowly turned her head to look at me. Then she gave me a radiant smile— one of the most beautiful smiles I had ever seen. She couldn't speak, but all the power of her love flowed into me from her eyes, her face and her brilliant smile. Afterward, she slowly and silently turned her head back onto the pillow and closed her eyes to rest. My mother passed away the next day. She had left me with one last remembrance: her sweet and tender smile was the greatest gift she could have given me.

A smile should be sincere and should be made with your whole face—your eyes, your lips and your mouth. A big smile shows you care, you are enthusiastic, and that you are trustworthy.

Let's have some fun. I am going to show you how to smile with your whole face. First, stand in front of a mirror and watch yourself do this exercise. Second, warm up by moving your lips back and forth as if you are quickly kissing a roomful of people.

Do it fast until it burns! Now raise your eyebrows and smile with your mouth at the same time. It's just like laughing and smiling all at once. Doing this little exercise every morning will keep your "kisser" in shape and it will keep you laughing inside all day long.

You brighten up your whole world when you give yourself and others the gift of smiling.

✿ 25 ✿
Alcatraz

A call came from the Women's Detention Center, asking if I would provide some life skills training for the women who were about to be released from prison. All the women at some point would be going back into society—except for the few inmates who were in for capital offenses, such as the petite blonde inmate who was serving a life sentence for disassembling her husband with a sharp object.

While the caller talked to me on the phone, all kinds of thoughts went through my mind. I remembered the horrible things I had seen in the movies about prisons, like The Birdman of Alcatraz, and my vision of prison was pretty awful. I wondered what kinds of situations and inmates I might encounter at this place. Being asked to do a program in a women's prison also made me a little nervous, I had to admit, but since I was . . . and still am . . . in the business of helping people (all kinds of people with all kinds of problems), I accepted this assignment.

After going through the prison's security process, I was then given a tour of the facilities. To my surprise, it was clean and modern and nothing at all like I had seen in the old Hollywood "B" movies about prisons, except for the clanging of the barred metal doors that slammed shut with a loud and hollow sound when they locked behind me. Every time those metal doors closed behind me, I felt a wave of despair for those women who would not be able to just walk out of the building that day as I would later do. I reminded myself that my program must be uplifting and also useful to these women, and a negative or despairing attitude from me feeling sad would surely interfere with those results. So I pulled myself together and began my presentation before my "captive" crowd of listeners.

Regardless of whatever kind of workshop I present, with my natural love of laughter, I can't help throwing something funny and humorous into my programs. For example, I told the women that day not to take my advice literally when I said, "Let's take a break!" They got a kick out of that one. Several of the women told me later that my presentation was going to help them prepare for reentering society after their release from prison.

After the seminar, I sat down with some of the women and listened as they talked about their childhood experiences. Many inmates had a somber story to tell of growing up in families broken by alcohol, violence, and divorce. Some told of being beaten and sexually abused. I could see the pain and anger in the eyes of these women and heard them tell me about their fears and misgivings of ever blending back into society and having a really happy life. Though they had been placed in the detention center for a variety of reasons— crimes of theft, violence, fraud, embezzlement, drugs, etc.—my heart went out to each one of them. I empathized with the pain and suffering they had endured as children and with the circumstances that had set them on a course of destructive behavior, defeat and sorrow as adults.

Even today, the stories of these women never seem to escape me. My own childhood was less than ideal, and life has posed some tremendous obstacles in my path along the way. But I am still extremely grateful for my numerous blessings and for my learned resourcefulness that helped me make a happy and satisfying life for myself.

Some people's burdens are much greater than ours.

*"The only thing we have to
fear is fear itself."*
—*Eleanor Roosevelt*

🦋 26 🦋

The Boogeyman

With so much on the news these days about a
spiraling crime rate and about women having
to learn to protect themselves, I decided to attend a
self-defense class on how to defend myself from the
"Boogeyman." The course instructor said most
"Boogeymen" attack people who act like they are
afraid or who seem to lack confidence. That's why,
if I am walking alone at night, I keep telling myself
how important it is to project power and confidence through my body language.

One dark evening as I walked a few blocks to my
car after a late meeting, I hurried along the deserted
street, my head still reeling with all the dire things
the self-defense instructor had drummed into my
mind. Then, a noise broke into my thoughts—a
noise that nearly scared me half to death! The trees
made shadows from the streetlights onto the sidewalk and the night became spookier and spookier as
I squared back my shoulders and tried to walk with
more determination—in heels! I was not going to
be a scaredy cat, but my heart was pounding! Then
I heard it again. It sounded like someone or something was following me! Swish! Swish! Swish!

I stood up straighter, clutched my purse under my arm and tried with all my might to project power, just like the instructor had said to do, but it didn't seem to alleviate my fear at all! Swish! Swish! Swish! I heard it again and I kept walking, but faster now—I was almost trotting. The noise—whoever or whatever it was—was keeping pace with me!

My heart pounded so loudly now I thought it would jump out of my chest, and I just knew I'd be mincemeat if the "Boogeyman" would catch up with me. "This is stupid!" I thought. I had just spent an hour-and-a-half learning to be more physically assertive and aware and here I was cowering on a dark street while being pursued by a nameless, faceless "Boogeyman." I dug down deep and pulled up a bunch of self-confidence, and took a huge breath. Trying to scare this stalker, I went into my fake karate stance and chopped at the darkness as I screamed, "I've got a black belt in karate!" I swung my arms out in front of me and crouched in what I thought was a most menacing way, as I kicked out and yelled, "Yah! Yah! Yah!" There was silence.

I held my karate stance, still breathing hard as I stared into the night. Nothing. Huh! I really impressed myself, if I'd done nothing else. My stalker had apparently disappeared. Whoooo! I let out a big breath and turned into the direction of my parked car. "Swish! Swish! Swish!" The noise again, but this time a little slower and not quite so loud. "Swish." Then I realized the source of my fear and flight. It was my pantyhose rubbing together! The mystery noise wasn't the "Boogeyman" after all! After I got in my car, I laughed at my fear and foolishness and then started the engine to drive home.

It is amazing how fear can sometimes ignite our imagination! We must remember to not let fear—imagined or real—control our lives.

The next time I am taking a walk and hear a "swishing" sound, I will first check to see if it is my pantyhose making the noise before I go into a complete panic.

Check out all the facts before letting fear control your life.

Dr. Klucko to the rescue.

Dr. Klucko,
My Featherless Friend

After doing a full-day seminar in Boston, I was very tired and I literally fell into my seat on the airplane. I got settled and buckled in as I listened to the pilot announce with deep regret that the plane unfortunately had mechanical problems. We would all have to disembark and go back to the terminal until the situation could be fixed. I felt like a rag doll who was losing some of her stuffing as I drearily gathered my belongings and trekked back to the terminal with the rest of the weary passengers.

Needless to say, no one was in a very chipper mood back inside the terminal, and I could feel the faint strains of a headache coming on. I rummaged through my briefcase for a bottle of pain reliever when my hand closed around the bumpy neck of my faithful friend and companion—the staple ingredient for all my humor seminars—my pale and hairless fair and fowl friend who travels with me everywhere—my rubber chicken! It was Dr. Klucko! I chuckled and thought that instead of the aspirin I should take a little of the advice I am known to give to others: "When you are tired and over-stressed, always carry something with you that has the power to remind you to laugh!"

Okay, Dr. Klucko—to the rescue! Do your stuff, Doctor! I placed my rubber chicken friend inside my open briefcase and then closed it so that just his long neck and red beak protruded at one end and his yellow clawed feet stuck out at the other. I walked through the crowded terminal that was filled with disgruntled and travel-worn passengers, and Dr. Klucko flopped along with me working his magic as I detected here-and-there little titters, timid "tee hees," and bold guffaws in my wake. Something amazing was happening, and it was not only happening to me! As I paraded up and down the long hallways, I sensed that the air was lighter with laughter, and that moods were lifting all around me. Dr. Klucko, my silly friend, had dispatched my own headache, as well as lifted the pervasive bad moods all around me. This "funky little chicken" had provided some lighthearted moments for many stranded air travelers and he managed to reenergize me enough to endure a long night in the airport terminal.

We all need to create a basket or bucket filled with fun things to make us laugh both at home and in our workplace. My "bucket of fun" not only contains my pal, Dr. Klucko, but also red rubber clown noses, funny hats, de-stress squeeze balls, a pair of eyeglasses complete with a big nose and "Groucho" eyebrows, whistles, toys, etc. I continually add fun things to my humor bucket that remind me to laugh when life seems a little grim. I also clip cartoons out of the newspaper. I have entertaining and witty cards posted on my bulletin board, a huge library of humor books, and comedy audio and video tapes to boost my mood when needed. At the office, dear Dr. Klucko perches on top of my computer and helps me de-stress when I am having one of those difficult times like trying to get online with the Internet. My office is not an ordinary office, but instead it is a joyful place that reminds me daily that I must "lighten up!" As a result, not only do I absolutely love what I do, but I am also more productive, more creative, and more energetic.

To de-stress, create your own fun environment at home and in your workplace.

"A life spent in making mistakes is not only more honorable but more useful than a life spent in doing nothing."
—George Bernard Shaw

28

Let the Beatings Begin

If there's anything that will give you wrinkles for sure, it is making a mistake and then emotionally beating yourself up for days, weeks, months and even years!

When I was in high school, I almost failed my driver's test. I couldn't parallel park to save my life, and over the years and even now this simple little skill still causes me a tremendous amount of stress. But despite my parallel parking phobia, I refuse to let it get me down. Years ago I purchased a large white car and showed it off to my friends, neighbors, and everyone one who was interested. Those who knew my lack of talent in parallel parking wondered why I bought such a big car, but with my "Can Do" attitude, I knew, Yes! I knew I could do it!—someday.

The first day I drove to work with my new big white car I tried parking in a space on the street near my office. After 10 minutes of going in, going out, going in and going out some more I stopped in frustration. I got out of my car to look at the parking space from a different perspective. Lo and behold, my back wheel had jumped up on the curb and my front wheel was wedged among some bright red geraniums in a planter box on the sidewalk. People passing by on the street pointed at my car and laughed.

Feeling defeated and upset I stomped across the street, grumbling, "I'll never be able to parallel park." Then before I walked into my office, I took one last look at my car. I broke out laughing.

"RuthKay," I declared with confidence, "Look at the positive side. There's no one in this city, state, or the whole United States who could park a car like that!"

Learn and grow from your mistakes, but don't forget to laugh.

29

The Stripper's Song

Isee perfectly poised women who have the unique ability to take something like a plain dress or suit and make it a fabulous fashion statement by accessorizing with a scarf. They can actually wear a scarf on one shoulder, walk around the room with such off-hand ease, and have the scarf stay in place the entire evening. I do not possess this talent. On the contrary, my scarves have a tendency to just "disappear."

Years ago, I used to teach an evening course entitled "Successful Sales Skills" at a local community college. I wanted to emphasize to the class that it was important to project an aura of power, seriousness and responsibility. I also wanted to make a good impression, so I wore a business suit and accented it brightly with a beautiful, red, silk scarf (silently praying the scarf would stay in place). In the first session of this course, we discussed the importance of proper business behavior, dress and etiquette.

We also discussed things such as avoiding making off-color remarks or jokes and being aware of image and body language.

Toward the end of the session, I nonchalantly touched the collar area of my suit to be sure my silk scarf was still in place. With some unease, I felt only my bare neck—my scarf was gone! I absently patted my neck and shoulder and glanced frantically around the floor for the bright scarf, all the while continuing to talk to my students. I thought the class was completely unaware of my predicament and was not observing my search. Then I glanced down and saw that the scarf had somehow wiggled its way down inside my suit leaving only a little red silk corner sticking out between the second and third buttons of my jacket. I grabbed the corner of the scarf furtively with one hand and started pulling it out in short jerks as I continued to speak. Suddenly one of the men in the class began singing the "Stripper's Song" and soon the whole class joined in, laughing at me.

Here we were, talking about proper business image and behavior, and the entire class was singing the "Stripper's Song!" I was flushed with humiliation and I felt like hiding under the big desk in the front of the room. My dignity was completely flattened.

Maybe they would just all leave and go home, I thought. My face felt hot. I took a deep breath and paused a few seconds to regain my composure, but once I saw the humor in the situation, I also joined in the laughter. As I laughed with my class about this comical situation, something powerful happened to me. I learned how to laugh at myself!

In this ever-changing, stressful world, we need to be open and willing to laugh at ourselves. The grins on my students' faces were telling me that they identified with my distress and they liked me all the more for laughing with them about it. As the great actress Ethel Barrymore once said, "You grow up the day you have your first laugh—at yourself."

Don't take yourself so seriously. Be willing to laugh at yourself.

*"Those who do not know
how to weep with their whole
heart do not know how to
laugh either."*
—Golda Meir

30

Falling Undies

D id you ever have one of those days that started out with little irritations that steadily progressed until the end of day seemed like a hopeless mountain of mess? On my way to a presentation for a group of educators in Colorado Springs, Colorado, things started going wrong even before I got out of my driveway. First my garage door opener wouldn't work, so I had to get out of the car and pull hard to close the heavy door, breaking two fingernails. Darn! I had just had a manicure the day before. Backing the car out of the driveway, I realized my skirt was caught in the door. My skirt was crinkled and smudged with dirt, but there was no time to change clothes. Then, I had a flat tire part way between Denver and Colorado Springs. There I was, all alone on a busy freeway. This was before cell phones were so readily available and there was no help in sight and no way of contacting anyone. The only solution I thought was to start walking back towards Denver to a convenience store I had passed along the way in hopes of calling for road assistance.

A cold wind was blowing and I was dressed in a light cotton summer outfit. It had been so warm when I left my house in Denver. Now, it was starting to rain, and I dreaded the walk ahead of me. After walking for what seemed like several miles, a young man from a utility company pulled over and offered me a ride. We drove back to a convenience store in south Denver where I called a towing service. Soon a man with a tow truck arrived and told me to hop in. We headed back down the highway while I gave him directions to my car.

Once we got to my car, the tow truck man asked me what I thought was an unusual question. "Ma'am do you have a donut?" he asked. Red-faced, I apologized and said if I had known he was hungry, I would have bought some donuts at the convenience store to bring with us. He looked at me, paused for a second, and then started to laugh. He was referring to a little tire that should be in the trunk of my car. He changed the tire and then I drove to Colorado Springs on three tires and a "donut."

Finally, it was late afternoon when I arrived at the beautiful hotel where I would be giving my presentation the next day. Any one of the elegant people at the cocktail party going on in the hotel lobby could tell by my appearance that day that I wasn't part of their upscale scene. I had started the morning out looking bandbox fresh, but since I had walked in the wind and rain down the highway, my crisp look had disappeared long ago. I looked more like a ghost at a Halloween party than a business traveler. My clothes looked like they'd been slept in and the wind had tousled my hair into a greasy, stringy mop. I noticed some of the people from the maintenance department staring at my greasy, oily hair and they looked like they wished they could have just turned me upside down and used my head to shine the floors in the ballroom.

Then a nice young man at the hotel reservations desk noticed my disheveled state and came to my rescue. He proceeded to help me with my bags and he hung the clothes I had brought on the luggage rack. He led the way to the elevator as I trudged along behind—no makeup, hair plastered down around my face, and practically dragging my purse and briefcase, as well as my spirit. This little parade we made—the bellboy, my luggage, and me—was quite a sight for all the well-heeled and smartly attired hotel guests to see. On my way to the elevator, I had to walk through yet another group of chic people who were having a private party. When we were halfway through the crowd, I noticed something had slipped down and out of the leg of my slacks that were hanging on the luggage cart. You see, the hotel had a cobblestone floor which made the cart vibrate as we moved along, causing my undies that were apparently hiding inside the garment to slide out of one leg of my hanging slacks and gently parachuted to the floor. Just then, I remembered that the last time I had worn those slacks I had removed the slacks and my undies in one swoop. Now the undies were slowly, but surely drifting out of the pant leg where they had been stashed and they were making a "peek-a-boo" entrance down, onto the floor of the hotel ballroom right in front of my horrified eyes!

There I was standing in the middle of this swanky party with a pair of my big cotton undies, which resembled a miniature parachute, now resting at my feet. I froze for a millisecond. I felt like all eyes were on me as I stooped down and casually picked up the offending unmentionables and stuffed them in my pocket. Next I got back in step and jauntily followed the bellboy to the elevator, not even glancing back at the astonished crowd. I hoped none of those people would be attending my presentation the next day.

When I finally got safely inside my hotel room, I flopped on the bed with fatigue and mortification flooding my senses. What a day! Since I hadn't had anything at all to eat since early that morning, my stomach let me know how hungry I was. Because it was so late when I called room service, I was informed that the kitchen was now closed.

Well, that was the last straw! The tears started to flow. After all of the negative events that day, I threw myself on the bed and cried, howled and pounded the pillows with my fists for what seemed like an eternity. This string of stresses created a burgeoning dam inside me, and I felt relieved after opening the floodgates. Only then did I feel I could face another day . . . and have confidence I could make it a wrinkle-free one.

Give yourself permission to cry—it's okay.

"Hello, my little friends. Let me tell you a story."

❦ *31* ❦
Butterflies and Squirrels

After moving six times in seven years, I was not looking forward to another change. But I had to move back to Colorado Springs from a rented apartment in Denver so I could sell my house in the Springs. After days of packing, I drove from Denver to Colorado Springs and waited several hours for the moving truck to arrive. Since the weather was beautiful, I decided to sit on the bench in the backyard. I was exhausted and dreading the thought of unpacking, of putting my house on the market, and also having to get ready for a business trip in a few days. I felt overwhelmed and was in the process of having a major "pity party."

From out of nowhere, a husky squirrel appeared and parked himself at my feet. He sat up on his hind legs and rubbed his paws together looking at me all the while. Someone told me a long time ago that when you are upset you should talk to God's little creatures. I found myself telling him about all the hassles I was going through. He appeared like he was really listening to me; however, in reality I knew he probably just wanted me to feed him. As I talked on and on to him, and I guess to myself, I decided that things weren't really so terrible after all and maybe I would just cancel the "pity party." Immediately I felt better. The next morning when I went out into the back yard, there stood my furry friend waiting to greet me. He had something in his mouth that looked like a muffin, so I called him, (what else?) "Muffin."

All that year, whenever I found myself stressed or discouraged, I would go out to the backyard to find "Muffin" waiting for me to share some peanuts and a little conversation. He never argued. He never scolded. He never tried to solve or fix my problems. He just listened. He became quite a comfort to me and became my confidant.

When my house finally sold and I moved back to Denver, I faced the familiar, but draining task of unpacking plus getting ready for an important program for a Fortune 500 company. In my nervousness, I went for a walk, looking to meet another "Muffin" in the park that I could visit with. Instead, that day I encountered a beautiful butterfly—bright yellow with black trim on her wings that glinted with iridescent colors in the sun. She fluttered her wings and circled around me. This was magical! I felt like a three-year-old seeing a butterfly for the very first time. I found myself twirling in a circle after her, laughing, and talking to this beautiful butterfly. Then she stopped as if to say, "It's been fun, sweetheart, and I wish you well, but I must be on my way." As she flew off, the pleasure I received from this brief and wondrous encounter with this exquisite creature was truly indescribable.

As I think about this encounter, I am in awe of how God's creatures and His majestic beauties of nature have helped me many times through stressful changes and have brought renewed joy into my life.

When having a pity party, take a walk, commune with nature, and talk to God's wonderful creatures.

*"Remember always that
you have not only
the right to be an
individual, you have an
obligation to be one.
You cannot make any
useful contributions in life
unless you do this."
—Eleanor Roosevelt*

❦ 32 ❦
Moneyless in Colorado

My mother gave me a lot of advice when I was growing up. Some of it stuck and some of it didn't, but two things I will always remember: the first was to not lose my individuality, and the second was to rely on myself, and not someone else, to take care of me. Those two guidelines have helped me throughout my life.

After living in the same small town all of my life, I decided to move to Colorado Springs, Colorado, after my divorce. All of a sudden I was newly single and living alone in a big city and I felt like I was on an emotional roller coaster. One minute I was overwhelmed and full of fear, and the next minute I was full of confidence and felt an exhilarating sense of freedom. I was excited and optimistic about my new life alone in Colorado and about my future. I settled into my new townhouse and started preparing for some important training programs I had scheduled with two major corporations.

One morning, however, I got a call that really dampened my enthusiasm. One of the training sessions for a big company in Seattle had been canceled due to company budget cuts. Although I was disappointed, I knew that everything would be all right because I had another substantial program coming up and that one would surely offset the loss of the first job. But the very next day, the manager from the second organization called to tell me their company had been sold, and he was forced to cancel my training program for the time being. That's when I went into a complete panic. There I was in a strange city all alone, my two biggest programs had just been canceled, and this had made a major dent in my financial plans. I was almost out of money! My fear factory was really working overtime.

I learned a long time ago that when the going gets tough, the tough go shopping! So, off to the grocery store I went to buy a little comfort in the form of ice cream, candy, and donuts. As I got out of the car to go into the store, I noticed a nice looking gentleman also getting out of his car—a shiny, new Jaguar. Oooh! I also noticed he wasn't wearing a wedding band.

At the checkout counter to my delighted surprise, the handsome "Jaguar" gentleman was standing in line right in front of me. As I waited for the line to move, my imagination soared. This good-looking, well-to-do guy was not only attractive, but he could also be the solution to my financial crisis! But, how could I get his attention?

Maybe I could shove my king-sized Tootsie Roll into his back and say, "Don't move! Today you are getting married!" My comedic fantasy continued. I would then order the security guard to marry us, the clerks would be our witnesses, and we would all meet in the bakery department for cake and punch to celebrate the nuptials!

"Ma'am, Ma'am! MAY I HELP YOU?!" Suddenly a loud voice broke into my daze and I realized it was my turn to check out. All the other customers were staring at me quizzically as I stood there embarrassed, holding my sugary purchases. I grinned at them apologetically and moved up to the register. The "Jaguar" gentleman had already finished paying for his few groceries and had left the store. My mother's old advice now echoed in my head, "RuthKay, never depend on someone else to take care of you." It was fun for just a minute to entertain a silly fantasy of "Mr. Rich and Wonderful" sweeping me up and off in his new Jaguar and taking all my money problems away, but I knew it was just an illusion I had created from my big fears of loss.

Today, I constantly reinforce Mom's good advice by adding one of my favorite affirmations, "If it is to be, it is up to me!" I knew that if I were to survive in my new life I had to come up with some innovative ideas to build my business and create my own prosperity in these new surroundings. I also reminded myself that with God's help, I will always have the ability and the strength within me to survive and to make my dreams come true.

In tough times, affirm the saying, "If it is to be, it is up to me!"

"So, you want to play, eh?"

33

Bumblebees and Basketballs

Books are a passion of mine, and I own hundreds of them. One afternoon I was looking for one special book and I just happened to run across my old workbook on "Goal Setting." It had been a long time since I had set some new goals for myself and I mused, well maybe that was why my life felt like it was sort of at a standstill lately.

After being deep in thought for awhile, I happened to look up above me and there was the most intimidating and meanest-looking bumblebee that I had ever seen. From as far back as I could remember, I have always had an irrational fear of bees and I'm still scared of them! I grabbed a newspaper, rolled it up to use as a "bee-swatter," and I was now armed.

But, this overly confident little critter knew that he had me on the run as he would dive down and then soar up again and again way out of my reach in the high cathedral ceilings of my townhouse. I think he really liked teasing me. He would fly down low and when I took a swat at him, he would buzz right up to the ceiling again. This went on for some time and I thought he seemed to be making a game of this and was probably laughing his little antennas off at me cowering in fear. I needed a solution to this problem if I was ever going to get any reading done that day. Hey! I thought. Here was a small goal I could actually set one that could probably be accomplished that very afternoon. I decided my goal was to put the ol' bee's lights out, but first I needed a plan of action. Because the ceiling was so high I had to find something I could use to reach the bee. Jumping up and dancing around in my living room had given me a bright idea. I could use my old basketball out in the garage. I used to be on the all-star basketball team in high school and in college and I still had my favorite basketball.

After a long search for it, I brought it inside and I had a lot of fun in my living room "basketball court" taking practice shots at the bee and pretending to make a basket each time I threw the ball up close to him. I missed hitting him several times, but it didn't discourage me.

Since I am a very competitive person, I remained determined that this pesky black-and-yellow striped insect would not get the best of me. I tossed the basketball up several more times, but still continued to miss making contact with the bee. Then I made a tremendous Michael Jordan leap and hurled the basketball up one more time in the bee's direction. It knocked him out of the air and he fell to the floor like a heavy sack of honey onto the soft carpet below. A quick scoop up with a Kleenex and "Buzz the bee" was out the back door, and we were both safe. I cheered, "Yahoo! I won! I did it! Yes!" and I jumped high in the air and clapped my hands.

Later that evening I wondered why I had such an exhilarating feeling of victory over such a really tiny insect problem. I mean, all I did was smack a bee and put him back outside where he belonged. But, then it dawned on me! That afternoon I had actually achieved a real goal (albeit a small one) and I had those same euphoric feelings of victory and accomplishment as I'd had in the past when I had reached one of my larger goals.

This unusual experience and my unique solution with the bee and the basketball helped me remember how exciting life can be when I set and achieve my goals. In order to get my life back on track, I knew I must start right away to set some goals for every area of my life—spiritual, physical, emotional, financial, family and career. But first, I needed to write down those goals, identify the obstacles, set target dates, develop plans of action, and visualize myself succeeding. I also needed to ask the experts for advice along the way. I knew that by following this plan, my life would soon become satisfying again and it would take on a whole new meaning.

When you set goals, your life will become more fulfilling.

🦋 *34* 🦋
What Next?

I had no idea when I awoke on that gorgeous Saturday morning that I would be faced with some pretty unusual situations before the day was through. First, I called my good friend Wanda and invited her over for lunch. As we were chatting away, I told her about my plans for a house-warming party. I was finally settled in my new townhouse and was eager to see all my friends I hadn't seen for awhile. I was finished at last with unpacking, and now I wanted some fun and diversion.

Over the years I have learned that whatever happens in my mind will also happen in time. This time, however, it happened much more quickly than I ever expected! As Wanda and I were discussing plans for the house-warming party, I thought I smelled something burning, and asked her if she smelled smoke? Yes, she did, and like hound dogs on the hunt, we relentlessly sniffed everywhere until I finally discovered that there was smoke coming from one of the switch plates on my living room wall.

Could this be a serious problem and would my switch plate soon erupt in flames? Well, how was I to know? So, I called 911 emergency to ask if this could be a potential fire hazard, and before long two fire trucks with howling sirens and blazing lights came to a screeching halt right in front of my townhouse. Wow! Six hunky and determined firemen ran briskly through my front door and into the living room to put out the big "fire."

It seemed that the entire Fire Department was immediately responding to my question to the 911 operator, but this wasn't exactly what I'd had in mind. After all, I had only wanted some information, but calling the 911 emergency number and giving my address had then brought a whole team in response to my smoky little problem. Oh, the firemen were wonderful! They checked out my entire house and found everything in good order except for the smoking switch plate in the living room. They explained to me that one of the electrical wires behind the switch plate was completely worn and that this was the cause of the smoke. Then they wound some black electrical tape around the unprotected wire, telling me that it was only a temporary measure and that I must get an electrician in to correct the problem very soon. I thanked these handsome "knights" in fireman-suited "armor" and sent them on their way.

Gosh! What excitement, and it was only two o'clock in the afternoon. I could tell by the fatigued look on Wanda's face, that she'd had about all the excitement she could stand for one day and was looking forward to going home to recuperate. "We could plan a party another time," she said.

Later, alone in my quiet house, I thought, "Gee, what next? Now what should I do with the rest of this day?" Well, I decided to run some errands, and being true to my philosophy of always making happy events out of dull routines, I first treated myself to a chocolate soda at a nearby ice cream shop before stopping to get my mail at the privately-owned postal center where I rented a mailbox.

I got there when it was after-hours for the retail part of the store. No one was around and the place was empty, so I just let myself in with my own key provided to me as a postal customer at the store. The door unlocked easily and I went inside and retrieved my mail. Lots of mail here to answer, I thought, as I gathered up my things to leave the store and head back home.

I tugged and tugged at the front door to the store, but it just wouldn't budge. I had no trouble at all getting into the store, but getting out was another matter altogether! I banged on the glass door and shook it by the handle whenever anyone walked by outside, but the passersby just ignored me as they scurried on down the sidewalk. What could I do? Somehow I just had to get out of there!

Fortunately, there was a phone inside the store next to the mailboxes for the use of postal customers and I realized my only recourse was to call the emergency number 911 for the second time that day. Within almost no time at all, three black-and-white police cars pulled up in front of the store, sirens whining and red and blue lights flashing madly in the parking lot. This scene, of course, now attracted a lot of attention and quite a crowd of curious bystanders. If I had been on the outside looking in, I would have thought that someone had either broken into the store or that a sought-after criminal had finally been found.

I felt like a caged animal on display at the zoo, and I must have been quite a comical sight as I tried to scream at the top of my lungs through the thick glass door to all the people outside staring in at me. But my voice was muffled by the security glass, and I had to pantomime my situation. Finally, through my frantic gestures and with the police officers being able to lip-read, they realized I had not broken into the store, but I only wanted to break out instead!

The policemen told me to stay calm and they would send a locksmith and would have me released from my "postal prison" just in time to get home to see myself on the ten o'clock news.

What a day! That night I fell into bed totally exhausted. But, as I reflected back on the day's events, first with being rescued by the Fire Department and then later being released from "postal prison" by the "Boys In Blue," I had to laugh at the incredible and impossibly unexpected situations I had been faced with that day. All in all, I was really pleased with the way everything had finally worked out, and I was also pleased at how well I had handled the panic and stress as well.

Years before, I might have gone into a complete emotional tailspin instead when things went awry. If you had known me then you could have nicknamed me "Wilma Worry Wart" because I was obsessed with the "What ifs" in life. You know, all those self-defeating fear questions we ask ourselves, like, "What if I get sick and end up in the hospital?" and "What if I go broke?" and "What if I fail?" or "What if I'm a success and can't handle it?" and the worst "What if" of all, "What if I were ever to lose a loved one?"

Obsessing over the "What ifs" caused me to be afraid of taking any risks because of what could or would happen in the precarious and doubtful future.

This uncertainty always kept me on edge. I constantly agonized over things that required taking risks or making changes because I always asked myself, "What if?" I created the worst-case outcomes and I was sure I wouldn't be able to manage under stress when and if the time to act ever came.

Well, eventually each and every one of my "What ifs" actually happened, and as traumatic and soul-searing as each event was, with the help of the Lord and kind and loving people, I found the courage needed to cope with the tragic "What ifs" that life sent my way.

You never know what your future may bring. However, if you can develop the mindset that no matter what happens, your faith in God and your trust in yourself will carry you through, then you will have formed the strength of mind that will enable you to survive any tragedy that comes your way.

Expect life's unexpected events, and believe that you can handle them.

"Ma'am, please tell me I have the wrong address."

🦋 *35* 🦋
... And Then He Was Gone

All my friends were very concerned about me being alone after 28 years of a marriage that had just ended, so they decided to fix me up with a blind date, saying it would be a "fun" adventure for newly single me.

I hesitantly agreed to this and so the arrangements were made for me. After getting mostly ready for my date, I realized I had about an hour-and-a-half before the fellow would arrive to pick me up, and since I was scheduled to do a seminar on laughter the next day I decided to use my extra time to rehearse my program. I got into my costume—a big, fuzzy bathrobe with yellow "baby chick" slippers—and I put on my red clown nose, donned my wild purple wig and started rehearsing.

Everything went great until I heard the doorbell ring. Well, it must be my neighbor Kelly checking up on me, I thought, so I ran to the door looking a little like I was auditioning for the circus. I thought my friend Kelly, who was always fascinated by the humorous programs I presented, would get a big kick out of this particular costume, so I threw open my front door with a loud and musical, "Ta! Da!"

Unfortunately, it wasn't Kelly. Instead to my surprise, there "he" stood—my blind date! Oh! How I kind of wished he had actually been blind. That's when I realized that after returning from a seminar in California the day before, my watch was still on California Pacific time, which is, of course, an hour earlier than Colorado Mountain time.

I sheepishly asked my blind date to come in. He was a clean-cut, sort of buttoned-down, well-dressed and nice looking middle-aged man who introduced himself to me as Howard. He looked at me like he had just seen the scary character from the horror movie "Hannibal." Howard stepped cautiously inside my door and with a weak and somewhat shaky voice asked me if I were RuthKay and if this was the correct address. I could see by the expression on his face that he hoped I would say it wasn't. Quickly, I snatched off my rubber clown nose and purple wig and stuffed them into one of the big pockets of my oversized bathrobe with my rubber chicken gamely peeking out at Howard from the big pocket on the other side. "Oh, Howard, it's so nice to meet you," I said. "Won't you come in and have a seat while I just finish getting ready?"

Howard came in and delicately balanced himself on the edge of my sofa while I ran upstairs to my room to hurriedly put on the finishing touches to my hair and makeup. I searched frantically for a pair of pantyhose that didn't have a run in them.

Thank Heavens! I found an unopened package that read, "One Size Fits All." Quickly I ripped open the package and began pulling the nylon hose over my feet. I was huffing and puffing like I was trying to lift a house off the ground with my bare hands. Then, realizing that the "One Size Fits All" label really does NOT really fit "ALL," I grabbed a hold of the elastic waistband with two hands and jumped up and down hoping I would stretch the tiny hose enough to fit into them. Boy, was I wrong! Nothing I did could make them fit me.

Then I realized I had kept Howard waiting much too long, so with the crotch of my pantyhose creeping halfway down to my knees with every step I took, I put on my chic little black dress and went to greet him downstairs in the living room. Now, wearers of pantyhose know it is almost impossible to walk naturally with the crotch of your hose inching halfway down to your knees, and it is even more impossible to walk down a flight of stairs while tugging at a falling waistband. I had to keep a death grip on the banister just to keep from floundering down the stairs. To understand what this feels like (for those of you who have never worn pantyhose) just try tying a cord halfway between your waist and your knees so that your thighs will not move independently of one another, and then try walking down a flight of stairs.

Finally, I made my spectacular entrance down the stairs and into the living room where Howard watched me all the while with an uncertain smile on his face. "Oh, Howard, I'm so sorry to have kept you waiting," I said with a bright smile.

"Oh, uh, well, that's, uh, all right," he stammered. Just then I remembered I didn't have my purse and it was, well, of course, upstairs, so I told him I would be right back again in a jiffy.

Well, if slithering downstairs in pantyhose was difficult, hopping upstairs was even worse. I can only image what my backside looked like as I ascended once more to my room. Oh, how I wished I had an electric chair lift so I could have gracefully ridden up those stairs. In my bedroom, after locating my purse and taking another quick glance at my hair and makeup in the mirror, as well as one final and futile tug on the offending pantyhose, I heard the unmistakable sounds of my front door quietly closing and furtive footsteps fleeing down the sidewalk, a car door slamming, and . . . poof! He was gone!

As embarrassing and comical as my first foray into dating was, I nevertheless felt proud of myself for agreeing at all to date once again and to begin new relationships.

After all, beginning adventures can be scary; however, if you remain open-minded, you can learn and grow, and sometimes even get a chuckle from them!

Be open to new adventures.

❦ 36 ❦
Paint It Red!

Sitting in traffic one afternoon, I heard an old song on the car radio and I started to sing along, "Getting to know you, getting to know all about you." For the rest of the day I couldn't seem to get the song out of my head and I kept singing and humming it to myself.

That evening I had my own concert. I continued to sing the song at the top of my voice while dancing around in my living room. I often dance around to music as a way to get some fun exercise, but if anyone would have viewed this scene they would surely have called the men in the white jackets to take me away.

The words of that song seemed to penetrate my very being and I asked, "How well do I really know myself?" I decided to take a mini-journey of self-discovery, and I recalled the results of a personality test administered by one of my colleagues. One of the things I remember her saying was that I was very sensitive to my environment and that harmonious living and working conditions were extremely vital for me.

I had achieved a satisfying business environment by decorating my office in bright colors, which were stimulating and exciting to me, plus I used a lot of color in my brochures and other business materials. However, my home space was lacking my personal signature. The designer of my brochures had remarked on this right away as she met with me in my home. "RuthKay," she said, "I know how much you love color and I am just so surprised that I don't see much of it in your home!" I realized then that I had never given much thought to extending the bright color scheme into my home environment. Although I always loved color, I never really gave myself permission for my home decor to reflect the real "me." Unlike my office, my home didn't have my personal stamp. I realized then that I really did not spend much time at home, instead preferring to work long hours at the office. I felt like my home was drab and nothing drew me to spend a lot of time there.

I set to work to change my home and create an atmosphere that said, "Welcome home, RuthKay!" I spent weekends and holidays painting the interior a basic soft white, knowing I would accent with the bright colors I loved so much. In the kitchen, I added red trim around the counters, cheery red curtains, and other red and yellow accessories. My dining room featured one immense wall in bright sunny yellow that angled up sharply to the cathedral ceiling. I added a curio cabinet and put in it bowls, plates, glasses, and flowers in shades of red, yellow, blue, and green. Placing this curio cabinet in front of the yellow wall added just the perfect touch and my spirit rejoiced at this colorful sight.

I knew my old "baby-poop" green carpet would have to go. So, I replaced it with a dazzling plush royal blue carpet that is jewel-like in its beauty, but it also picks up lots of lint. In fact, I like to say that it picks up everything but men and money! My white curved sectional sofa was brought to life with a vibrant assortment of plump pillows in bright colors.

At last! My home environment now was really perfect for me until I noticed my two large, beige, ceramic lamps. They were colossal and were very expensive, but their drab color did absolutely nothing for this glorious new room. They also gave off perfect light and were placed in strategic places in the room where I needed light, but what could I do about their awful color?

Then it dawned on me one Saturday morning as I stood in my kitchen sipping hot chocolate. I came up with an idea of painting those two lamps bright red! The lamps would be dominant items in my living room because they were four feet high and forty inches in diameter, and I hesitated to take on such a complicated refinishing project. But the lure of having brilliant color was too much to resist. I pulled out the can of leftover red paint that I'd used on the red trim in my kitchen and started right to work. The lamps looked regal and absolutely stunning in red! Now, every time I walk into my kitchen, living room, dining room and my entire house I am completely thrilled and satisfied that it all is a true reflection of me. I feel in awe of the power of beautiful, bright colors and they give me energy and joy.

I was a little nervous having my friends come in to critique my house makeover, because they were not into decorating with bright colors. Most of their homes were done in tasteful, but quiet earth tones. I thought they might feel my house was too garish for their tastes and I feared they would tell me I'd made a big mistake. To my surprise every one of them said, "Oh, RuthKay, this is so 'you!' This is the 'real you!'" They were delighted for me, and it was nice to know that my friends recognized and celebrated the "real" me!

I encourage you to also go on a journey of self-discovery. A good place to start is by asking yourself, "What kind of environment really makes me feel happy, energized, and enthusiastic about life?" You might discover that the answer to your question has been hidden inside of you and is just waiting to surface.

Getting to know you
getting to know all about you!

🦋 37 🦋
Happy Times

Every so often I fly to Virginia to visit my son Darrin. He is a very handsome young man in his mid-thirties and is a successful architectural designer. And because I'm his mother, I, of course, feel entitled, if not required, like any mother does from time-to-time, to just "shape him up" a little.

In fact, when I start offering a little too much advice, Darrin will usually good-naturedly threaten to take me for a ride in the car and show me the little retirement home he talks about where I might just have to live out my old age, if I'm not careful. Just thinking about such a dull place like a nursing home gives me the "heebie-jeebies," but more importantly, I realize then that what he is saying is that I might need to lighten up on my advice.

Darrin lives in a beautifully decorated home filled with carefully selected artwork, rare books and tastefully expensive furniture. I wondered how important these material trappings were to him, and I asked, "If the house ever caught on fire, Darrin, out of all these beautiful things, what would you take with you as you dashed out the door?" To my surprise, he said he would take the pipe collection he has in a glass case in his living room. He said the majority of his pipes represent wonderful memories of the places he has traveled around the world. But his most valued pipes in this collection are the ones given him by his father and his grandfather. Darrin has treasured memories connected with the special tobacco aromas that cause him to reflect back on his times with his Grandpa Pete, who also smoked a pipe. Whenever Darrin smokes the same blend of tobacco as his Grandpa did, the tobacco aroma reminds him of the fun times they had during their summers together in Wyoming.

After our reflective conversation, I knew that even though Darrin was an intensely career-minded guy, he was also just as sentimental and as tender-hearted as I was, and that this loving man was truly his mother's son.

Whenever something happens in my life that touches my heart, I try to buy a special treasure for my home just to keep the precious memory alive. Here's an example of one summer day with my ailing mother. One warm and sunny afternoon I took my mother for a ride in the country. Although she was very ill from a chemotherapy treatment for cancer, the ride helped her focus on the beautiful scenery and our talk drifted to the memorable times we'd had in the past.

And since a perfect day like this one would probably never happen again with her, I wanted to remember that afternoon forever. On our way home, I stopped by a flower shop and bought two little baskets filled with brightly-colored silk flowers that I later placed on my dining room table. My mother passed away six months later. Now, every time I look at these charming baskets of flowers, I remember that beautiful and priceless afternoon I shared with her.

To relive times that you have cherished with your family or friends, find something unique such as a beautiful rock, driftwood, or seashells, or buy something special and place it in your home or office. On a gloomy day, these keepsakes will help you remember happier times and will also renew your spirit.

Collect special treasures to remind you of happy times.

"A keen sense of humor helps us to tolerate the unpleasant, overcome the unexpected, and outlast the unbearable."
—Reverend Billy Graham

🦋 38 🦋
When Life Hurts

On September 1, 2000, my vivacious and beautiful daughter, KarleyKay, and her husband were killed in a head-on car collision. The news of their deaths nearly ripped my heart right out of my body.

The funeral was especially difficult. Several friends and members of the family got up to reminisce and to share their own memories of the couple. Then it was my turn to speak. I have been a professional speaker for almost twenty years, but this was absolutely the most difficult presentation I ever had to make. First, I told a few heart-warming stories about KarleyKay and then I related an amusing event that my daughter had told me about two weeks before her death.

KarleyKay had worked for the University of Colorado Hospital. One dreary Monday morning, she phoned Carmelle, one of the nurses who was also her friend in the office down the hall, to tell her that she was really worried because she had a very unusual and serious-looking growth appear on her face. She asked Carmelle if she would please come right away to have a look at it. Carmelle was very concerned and she hung up the phone and hurried down the hall to KarleyKay's office where she zipped through the door. KarleyKay was seated at her desk and trying very hard to keep a straight face. She was wearing a big red rubber clown nose and a huge grin! They both laughed hysterically.

Although the people attending the funeral were, of course, grief-stricken, after hearing this light-hearted story that was so typical of KarleyKay, they couldn't keep themselves from laughing out loud right there in the chapel. My point was that I wanted all the people present at that solemn occasion who had come to honor KarleyKay's passing, to also remember my precious daughter as a lively and fun-loving human being who gave to and got so much from life. Many people commented to me after the service that while they listened to this funny story about KarleyKay while watching me up at the pulpit demonstrate her wearing the red clown nose, that the feeling of lightness in the midst of sorrow had helped them cope a lot better with her death.

Regardless of how much pain and suffering you are going through, laughter is always healing and very therapeutic, especially when life really hurts.

Remember, laughter is healing.

🦋 39 🦋
"Napmares"

Whenever I cook, whether I boil water, fry, or bake something, my kitchen usually ends up looking like a war zone. I always encourage people to stay out of the kitchen while I'm cooking, warning them it could be hazardous to their health! People laugh, thinking I am trying to be funny, until they walk in and see the edges of my baking mitts burnt to a crisp.

I had been dating Barry for awhile and decided it was finally time to invite this nice, rather shy man over for a home-cooked dinner. The first step was finding the recipe in one of my mother's old cookbooks for the French dish with a special sauce that had a name I couldn't pronounce. The second step was to go to the grocery store to buy the ingredients. I selected a fresh whole chicken and put it in my grocery cart and continued to buy other ingredients. Before I left the store, I realized that one chicken may not be enough. So I went back to the meat department and picked up another chicken. As I glanced at the label on the package which said "Stewing Hen," I thought, oh, so what? A chicken is just a chicken.

Whew! I'd forgotten that serious cooking was a lot of hard work. All that chopping and mincing and stirring! I was really beat, and since Barry wasn't due to arrive for three hours, I decided to take a short nap on the couch. The last thing I remember before dozing off was that I had been preparing dinner for Barry in the kitchen and making the dinner became part of my dream state.

In the dream I'd called a friend, who is also an excellent cook, for some culinary advice. She suggested that whatever I fixed I should be sure to add a little wine to enhance the flavors. I followed her suggestion and went to the store to buy a bottle of wine, came home, and poured the wine over the chicken and began to roast it. The aroma from the oven filled the house. I attributed this heavenly smell to the wine, so I decided to just take a sample from the bottle, but I ended up having way too many sips.

I'm not at all used to drinking wine, so I had no idea that even though it tasted so light and fruity it had a really high alcohol level. Yes, the wine was "high" and so was I, and by the time Barry arrived for dinner, I was feeling and acting a little giddy. He thought my being tipsy was amusing, and we both laughed at my carefree attitude. The wine made me lose all my nervousness about having to cook a gourmet dinner and be a super hostess. Yes! The evening was really going to be swell.

Suddenly, we heard a loud noise coming from the kitchen! It echoed like rapid gunfire . . . Bam! Bam! Bam! Bam! Bam! Bam! . . . like six or seven rifle shots going off in succession. Barry and I looked at each other; our eyes wide and our mouths open in surprise. No more laughter now as we crept cautiously toward the kitchen to peek in and investigate. We looked around, but couldn't see anything wrong. Then we glanced up and to our horror we saw the raw biscuit dough stuck on the ceiling. Then I remembered I had left a package of biscuits on top of the hot stove—the kind that the Pillsbury® Doughboy recommends. I had forgotten to remove the biscuit dough from its pressure-packed paper tubing and it was now splattered up above us. The ceiling looked like it was sprouting huge mushrooms. I had to think fast! If those biscuits stayed up there and dried, they would soon be permanent ceiling fixtures and would be an everlasting tribute to my culinary shortcomings. I turned to wide-eyed Barry, and said, "Quick! Run into the garage and get me a ladder!" Barry was kept busy while I ordered him around like a drill sergeant, "Climb up! Steady now, Barry! Yes, scrape off those biscuits. Get that big one over there in the corner . . . it's drying out already!" Barry moved around the kitchen climbing and cleaning and scraping as if this was an ordinary occurrence for him on a date night. What a guy!

Soon we were able to sit down again at the lovely table I had decorated with flowers and with the nice dinner (sans biscuits) I had prepared. Barry had apparently recovered from "Operation Biscuit Mission" and our conversation was again light as we began to eat dinner. I was having a difficult time with the piece of chicken on my plate. I just couldn't seem to cut into it. It was then that I realized that I had made a major mistake in buying this tough, old stewing hen and cooking it along with the fryer as though it was a fryer. Since both chickens looked exactly the same there was no telling the difference between the tender chicken and the stewing hen. With a stroke of luck, Barry's plate was filled with the tender chicken and mine held the tough old bird. After numerous attempts to discreetly sink my knife and fork into this impenetrable stewing hen, I finally just grabbed the piece of chicken by the leg and thigh and pulled them apart with one powerful yank. My left hand holding the drumstick smacked Barry's wine glass, knocking it over and sending a waterfall of dark, red wine down the front of his crisp white shirt and tie and into his lap. I could tell by his stunned look that I'd rendered him completely paralyzed. He never moved a muscle, never blinked, swallowed, or even took a breath. He just stared at me, as if he wondered what was he doing here in this house of horrors?

Well, as you can imagine, I was more than embarrassed. Profusely apologizing, I helped him stand up and I led him into the living room to watch a little TV to recover while I tried to think of what to do next. I had only known this sweet guy for a few months and after tonight's fiasco, he might decide to leave town with no forwarding address just to get away from me.

Soon Barry was settled and calm in the living room and interested in a TV show, so I excused myself to go back into the "war zone," I mean kitchen, and do something about preparing a dessert. I'd been so involved in the dinner menu and the cooking, and the wine tasting that I had completely forgotten to make any dessert. I searched my pantry shelves. Aha! An angel food cake mix. This can't be too difficult to pull off in a hurry, I thought. After all that had happened, I was hoping that a delicious, spongy angel food cake, served with a little ice cream or some fresh fruit, would make up for all my goofs.

Working fast, I stirred up the ingredients and poured the batter into an ancient angel food cake pan my mother had given me years before. I placed the cake in the oven to bake, whipped off my apron, and went out again to join Barry in the living room. "In just a little while, Barry, we'll have dessert," I told him, crinkling my nose and smiling. We sat down together in front of the TV and held hands.

About ten minutes later, just as Barry put his arm around my shoulder and smiled at me, we heard the ear-shattering sound of my smoke alarm piercing the air! "What now!?" I thought as we ran to the kitchen to see smoke billowing out of the oven door and up to the ceiling toward the jangling smoke alarm. Of course, what else? It was just another thing

I'd tried to cook. It was the cake! The battered 30-year-old angel food cake pan I used was bent on the bottom, which caused the cake batter to slowly ooze out all over the floor of the hot oven. Barry grabbed my potholders—a pair of charred and singed baking mitts that were survivors from previous kitchen disasters—and leaning in courageously through billowing smoke, he bent forward to lift out the charred cake pan from the oven. But, as he reached inside, the frayed oven mitt stuck on one of the hot electric coils and caught on fire. He jerked his arm out waving the flaming oven mitt in the air. Ouch!!!

I was panic-stricken! Why hadn't I invested in a fire extinguisher? I ran over and grabbed the sprayer from the kitchen sink. The sprayer hose wasn't long enough to reach the stove and my hands were really shaking badly as I sprayed Barry with water from head to toe. He stood in the middle of my kitchen staring at me as I held the sink sprayer. I stared back. His hair was plastered on his forehead and water dripped down his disbelieving face, while his arms hung lank at his sides, his hands still wearing the charred and now steamy oven mitts. I now had startled him beyond belief.

Suddenly, I awoke from this nightmare and I sat straight up on the couch, breathing hard and feeling a little dazed. Was that all a dream? It was so real! My heart was beating like a jackhammer and I was flushed and felt hot like I had been in the oven with the burning cake. I realized with relief that I just had a nightmare. No, since it was afternoon and I had just taken a nap, I guess it was really more like a "napmare"! Sighing a big sigh of happiness that I hadn't really ruined a French dinner, my kitchen, and a new relationship.

From time to time, I find myself laughing as I look back on all the bizarre things that happened in my "napmare" that afternoon. You could say I have a really interesting dream life! Since cooking often turns into a nightmare for me, I now always call out for pizza or Chinese food when I plan on inviting someone to my home for dinner. Many of my "napmares," and my night dreams, too, are made up of scenarios so far-fetched they have made me howl with laughter, so I decided it would be really fun to enter them into a dream journal. Now, whenever I have a particularly trying day, I can always read my journal for a little comic relief. It tickles my funny bone and before I know it, I can't remember what my stress was about.

Giggle your stress away with a journal filled with your funny dreams and comic waking experiences.

"I've got a new attitude!"

❦ 40 ❦
Groovin' and A' Movin'

Claiming to be the Number One "Shopaholic" in the world, there is always someone in my workshops who wants to challenge me and compete for my title. They do, that is, until they hear that I can actually bound from a moving car onto a mall's parking lot and get through a revolving department store door on a dead run in less than five minutes.

One afternoon I asked my good friend Elaine if she would like to go shopping, as the newspaper ads promised the biggest sale of the summer at all the mall stores. Since Elaine had just purchased a new car, she was eager to take me for a spin in it. As she slowly drove in front of the big department store entrance at the mall and busily searched for a parking space, I was really impatient to get inside and have a crack at those sales, so I said, "Elaine, I'll pop out and just meet you inside!" I opened the car door, swiftly jumped out of her car, and raced into the mall's spacious hallways, leaving Elaine sitting behind the wheel of her car with her mouth still forming a little "O" of amazement. As long-time shopping buddies, Elaine was used to me leaping out of the car while it was still moving, but it never ceased to astonish her.

I flat-footed it into a shoe store where a big sale was in progress and some really upbeat music was pulsing away from the store's sound system. For a minute I thought I'd run into a salsa club by mistake. Out from behind the counter came a really hip and handsome young man gyrating and grooving to the loud music as he danced toward me.

"Heeyyyy! Good lookin', how can I help you, ma'am?" he rapped out with a big smile while never missing a beat of the music. My mouth flew wide open with surprise—so wide, in fact, you probably could have thrown a cantaloupe into it. I was not accustomed to being treated this brashly by store clerks. His overly familiar attitude irritated me, but I kept my cool and smiled. I pointed to a pair of red, sling-back sandals that were on display in the front window. "I'd like to try on these in a size 6," I said, as business-like as I could manage to sound. The young clerk replied in rhyme, "Cut me some slack, and I'll be right back!" Well! I was more than a little exasperated, and my eyes followed him as he moved to the back of the store. His body moved in so many different directions at one time that I thought this guy might be a great candidate for chiropractic care.

In a few minutes, "Mr. Groovin' and Movin'" sales clerk returned still wiggling like a rap star on stage and he was wailing away in tune with the music being played. I guess he really likes his job, I thought to myself. He took the sandals out of the box and dropped them both onto the floor with deft movement and a "Yeah! All right!" and just kept on grooving. Well! What was this! I saw that he had brought me a size 9, not a size 6, so I handed them back to him and almost shouted, "This is the wrong size!" "Oooh, yeah!" he said and then he tossed the size 9 shoes up in the air, catching one behind his back and the other under his leg before he happily sauntered off, still grooving to the music as he went back to the storeroom to find the correct size. His next effort produced the correct size this time, but the wrong style—pumps, not sandals! Still grinning at me, he presented this pair of shoes with a flourish. This young man is just a little too happy, I thought, and I am a woman on a mis-sion—a shoe-shopping mission.

I was still waiting for my friend Elaine to show up after parking the car and I couldn't wait to tell her about this spacey shoe clerk. Where the heck was she? Where the heck was the shoe clerk? He had merrily gone off again to find me the red sandals and now he was nowhere in sight. I was very impatient and annoyed. I was a woman in a hurry and I wanted to shop! But I relaxed and counted to ten before the clerk returned so I could really blast him about his sales technique. The music boomed on and on. My foot was tapping, in annoyance, of course, but it was tapping, and my shoulders and upper body were moving in time to the music. I got up to look at a display in the center of the store and oh, yeah, the music was really getting to me now! I was groovin' and a' movin' with the beat. This was great!

The young clerk returned with more shoe boxes under his arm and a big grin on his face when he saw me swaying with the music. "Yeah, lady, that's it! You got it, lady. You got the moves!" he said as we moved and grooved around the glass display table. By this time, his happy and wacky attitude was contagious and I grinned, too. Although this guy never did find the right pair of shoes I wanted, his happy-go-lucky personality and the groovy music had done away with my anger and frustration. I was no longer impatient or uptight since I had decided to "go with the flow" of the beat. Music is life and this young man was joyfully filled with it. That day, I found out first hand what the experts say is true—music stimulates and soothes the emotional brain.

When you get uptight, groove to your favorite music.

❦ *41* ❦
Let's Play

After the loss of my beloved daughter, KarleyKay, in a tragic car accident, my life was understandably turned upside down. I do feel very fortunate though that she and I were always close and that we made a point of creating memorable traditions and memories that now live on in my heart. The traditions we had were full of fun, silliness and laughter. Yes, laughing, like stress, can also cause fine lines and wrinkles to appear, but what better way to show the world all the joy and happiness life has given you?

Although KarleyKay was in her early 30s, and I am halfway to 100 (plus a few years), when we got together we often acted like a couple of teenagers. We loved to talk about makeup and hairstyles, clothes, movies, work and just about everything. We even giggled and took votes on things like who was cuter, Tom Cruise or Mel Gibson?

Since we both loved to shop, KarleyKay and I went shopping together regularly, and our excursions evolved into traditions that were enjoyable and unforgettable. First, she would drive to my house, then hop into my car and I would drive us both to the mall. KarleyKay always joked that what she called my "dare devil" driving not only caused her stress, but also gave her premature wrinkles. She would grimace and grip the door handle tightly whenever I turned sharp corners and then she would pretend to try to stop the car by stomping on imaginary brakes from the passenger's side. Sometimes she would jokingly beg me to, "Please, please, Mom, stop the car!" and let her out so she could just take a taxi to the mall.

Our usual routine was to shop for a couple of hours and then stop for a gabfest and a great lunch at one of our favorite restaurants. To add to our fun day, we would play a little game. I would sit down on a mall bench while KarleyKay would sneak off to the candy store to buy some of my favorite chocolate bonbons with orange filling. I would pretend I didn't know she was gone and when she returned from her sweet errand, I would always act s-o-o-o-o surprised. Then I would give her a "high five" and ask if she had remembered to have the calories removed. The memory of our shopping "marathons," our happy lunches together, and this one favorite chocolate tradition makes me laugh and touches my heart still.

On one shopping excursion, we walked into a bookstore and we heard some romantic waltz music playing on the sound system. With a gleeful glint in her eye, KarleyKay quickly set her shopping bags aside and grabbed my hand, twirling me around the store like we were ballroom dance contestants. We dipped and glided in time with the music all around the bookstore to the amazement of many of the patrons.

KarleyKay's sense of fun and merriment was irrepressible and it spread throughout the quiet little store. Noses came up out of books and people turned to watch as we waltzed right by them.

We had very few "ordinary" days. KarleyKay always made a point of creating fun-filled traditions with me like the constant good-natured teasing about my driving, our shopping trips and lunches, and all of the spontaneously joyful things she did in her short life. I will always treasure these memorable traditions and the special times that I shared with my beautiful daughter.

Take time to have fun with your children, regardless of their ages, and create your own memorable traditions.

"It is one of the most beautiful compensations of this life that no man can sincerely try to help another without helping himself."
—*Ralph Waldo Emerson*

42

Experience a Miracle

It was the morning of a great workshop I had waited for. I was one of several speakers at a gathering featuring many of my own mentors and idols in the "positive thinking" movement. I couldn't wait to get there and be a part of it all. With my mind on a hundred different things, I hurriedly ran downstairs to load some of my presentation materials into the car. As I was going into the garage, I stepped down and turned my ankle. Hearing and feeling a "snap," I fell to the floor like a hundred pound bag of potatoes. The pain was almost unbearable; however, since this was one program I felt I simply could not miss, I stood up, dusted myself off and hobbled to the car. "Maybe it's not broken," I thought. "Maybe it's just a bad sprain." Oh, did it hurt!

My ankle was throbbing so badly that I cried as I drove all the way to my destination. Before I got out of the car, I took a peek at myself in the mirror. Tears had caused my mascara to run and smudge, and somehow I had also managed to smear my lipstick and a glob of it had ended up on my nose. I looked like a cross between a raccoon and Rudolph the Red-Nosed Reindeer! I couldn't help but grin a little and grimace at how goofy I looked. After mopping myself up, I hobbled to the place where people were now pouring in to find seats for this big program. I was scheduled to be the first speaker.

Whenever I hurt, sympathy from others always seems to help, and I sure got a lot of it from the meeting planners and the attendees when I arrived. I was trying to figure out how in the world I was going to stand on my feet for forty-five minutes with my ankle throbbing. I thought of all kinds of ideas. Maybe someone could hold me up during my presentation, kind of like a circus act. Or maybe someone could at least hold my ankle and squeeze it like a bandage while I dragged my "human tourniquet" around with me on the stage. Both of these scenarios made me laugh.

After hearing my name announced and the applause from the audience, a thousand eyes turned in my direction, and something very unusual started to happen. I do remember that my ankle was hurting when I stood up; however, when I began speaking, interacting and having fun with the audience, somehow I couldn't feel a thing! I walked all over the room during my presentation and my ankle didn't seem to hurt a bit. I had tons of energy. Was I having one of those out-of-body experiences that I'd heard so much about? After my presentation, I sat down to listen to several other speakers, and my ankle started to throb again. I could also see it was beginning to swell.

I have had many small (and even a few big) miracles in my life, but this was one of the most unusual things that had ever happened to me. After giving it a lot of thought, I realized that when I took my mind completely off myself and my pain, and instead focused entirely on the needs of the group looking and listening so attentively to me, the pain had just gone away.

In the years since then I have had occasions to test this. I found that whenever I was undergoing some kind of pain, grief, or trauma and I removed my thoughts from my own situation while projecting care, concern, and attention on others, that whatever the pain was—mental or physical—during that time, the pain temporarily subsides. If you find yourself going through some troubled times or perhaps you are having physical pain that cannot be attended to just then, try focusing on other people and their needs. You might have the same wonderful miracle happen to you that happened to me.

Focus on the needs of others and your pain may subside for a while.

"Find something to laugh about."
—*Maya Angelou*

❦ 43 ❦
Think Funny

During my climb up the corporate ladder, I received this valuable advice from my mentor: "Choose your battles carefully or you will be at war at all times." The same is true for those who suffer from stress. We must become very aware of what we allow to stress us or we will be distressed (and "at war" with ourselves) all the time.

In life there are some things we can control and some things we can't. So we need to learn early to adapt to the uncontrollable things. Foul weather, traffic jams, and a bad hair day can really take the starch out of your best plans to have everything go "just right." When you are faced with these little "wrinkles" in your day, you simply have to find some creative ways to smooth them out.

For example, elevators always unnerve me—not the elevators themselves, but some of the people who ride in them. Have you ever noticed when people get on the elevator they look right past you? They immediately back up against the wall and stare at the lighted number display or at the floor. This really bugs me, but I have developed ways to cope with it.

A good friend E-mailed me a list of silly things to do while on an elevator and I added several more of my own. By doing or just visualizing these funny activities while riding on an elevator, I can relieve my frustration. I encourage you to try some of these things, or even make up a few of your own:

- *Hand out breath mints.*
- *Bark or meow occasionally.*
- *Hop on the elevator and hop off.*
- *Pretend you are talking to your imaginary friend.*
- *Sing "Welcome To My World!" when people get on.*
- *When folks exit, shout, "Please! Please! Don't leave me!"*
- *When the elevator stops at each floor, cheer and say, "Yes! Yes! We made it!"*
- *Look deep into your purse or briefcase and inquire, "Got enough air in there?"*

When I tell people to try these wacky things, you should see the strange looks on their faces! They think I have lost my mind, and of course they do not want to appear to be "un-cool." Most people are afraid of making fools of themselves—and I get paid for it.

Remember, humor is contagious, and acting a little silly now and then is a great equalizer in situations such as being on an elevator, standing in a long line, or being stuck in traffic. You will lift your mood and you will cope much better with the stresses of the day.

Try funny tactics to cope with things you can't control.

❦ 44 ❦
Circle of Love

At a very early age I truly felt no one loved me. I have that same feeling at times to this day. I have always had a lot of friends and acquaintances, but I had never allowed myself to love or be loved too deeply. Even though my friends frequently told me they loved me, I didn't really hear them. I always had a hard time believing anyone really loved me. Something within me wanted to reject those three words: "I love you."

One of the tenets in my presentation on Staying Motivated is to accept a compliment when it is given. Most people are embarrassed when someone says something nice about them, so they tend to deny the compliment or shrug it off. I encourage people to listen carefully to the compliment, believe it, inhale it, savor it, hold it, mentally listen to it again and then swallow it so it can nurture them.

I enjoy receiving compliments and those favorable bits of feedback always nurture me.

Therefore, I have asked myself numerous times why can I accept a compliment, but not the loving words of friends? Through a lot of soul searching, I discovered that during my childhood the people who said they loved me would always hurt me through unkind acts and abusive words. This contradictory behavior led me to distrust those three words—"I love you"—and I closed my heart and mind to them. Consequently, I learned to ignore and mistrust love, which is the most valued compliment I could ever receive.

One evening like many times before, the thoughts and feelings of being unloved surfaced again. In an attempt to confront this problem, I poured a cup of tea, lit some candles, turned on some soft music, turned off the lights and sat on a big pillow on the floor. Then I visualized my friends circled around me. I mentally heard my dear friends, one by one, telling me they loved me. Pushing away my doubts, I opened my heart and mind to receive their precious utterances and let their words soak in. For the first time I truly accepted and believed the words "I love you" and I felt loved.

Since this exercise was so helpful, I now follow this routine whenever I am beginning to feel a little uncertain about myself or when those empty feelings about being unloved surface. This exercise reminds me to listen carefully to that greatest compliment of all when it is sincerely offered, and to accept it and believe it, so it can nurture me.

Open your mind and heart to the words "I love you" from true friends.

❦ 45 ❦
Group Strength

From my living room looking to the south I can see huge, old Cottonwood trees stretching toward the sky, fields of green grass, and a babbling brook inhabited by several ducks that regularly come there to swim and bask in the sun.

To the north, I can watch the birds eating from a feeder in a large pine tree. Many birds come to this feeder for their daily meal, and every once in a while I see a squirrel invading the bird feeder and gobbling up all of the seed. What amazes me is how the birds react to the squirrel. When they see him approach the feeder, they scatter.

Some birds fly away and others will just perch in nearby trees and small bushes to hang back and watch the squirrel raid their food supply. When I see this, I want to go out and shout to the birds, "Don't be afraid of the big, bad squirrel! You don't realize how much power you have. If all of you would band together, you would scare the birdseed right out of him and he would probably never return to terrorize you."

The same is true for people facing daunting issues. When we firmly believe in a cause worth

United we stand.

fighting for, we must all pull together to help make this a better world to live in.

The devastating events of the September 11th "Attack on America" has made all Americans feel threatened as we experienced an assault on U.S. citizens within our own country by an outside terrorist force. We could be like the birds—scatter, fear the bully and feel powerless. But when we band together, we are strong and our voices are heard. Together, we stand united against evil and terrorism. We are showing terrorists that we remain a strong, peace-loving people and we will not be pushed into a cowering position.

Let's band together to make a difference!

About the Author

RuthKay Petersen is an international motivational speaker, humorist, and entertainer. Through her keynote presentations on leadership, team building, customer service, change management and the power of laughter in the workplace, she has brought her entertaining messages to more than 1,800 audiences since she founded her business, Essentials For Success, in 1983. Essentials For Success was selected *Business of the Year* by the Small Business Administration. RuthKay received a special award of recognition from the Eighth United States Army, Korea for her outstanding performance at the BOSS Seminar at Camp Humphreys in Pyongtaek, South Korea.

Author of nationally published articles on *How To Stay Motivated In A Changing World* and *How To Add Laughter To Your Sales Success,* she has also produced audio and video tapes on the *Power of Laughter in Business.*

Her clients include MCI Telecommunications Corporation, Mercedes-Benz, AT&T, McDonald's, U.S. Air Force Academy, U.S. Army, Department of Defense, California Federal Bank, Vail Valley Business Women's Association, plus many more.

RuthKay's most popular programs include the following:
- *Motivation Magic!*
- *The Power of Laughter in Business*
- *How To Stay Motivated in a Changing Workplace*
- *How to Create a Fun Work Environment to Increase Morale and Productivity*
- *How to Add Laughter to Your Sales Success*
- *Beyond the Second Mile (The Power of Little Things in Business)*

Plus . . . A new soul-stirring program for women: **Anatomy of a Wrinkle: Fun and Inspirational Ways to Help Smooth Out the Wrinkles of Life**

If you would like to have RuthKay speak at your next event, please call 1-800 390-1993 or 303-221-7791, or visit her Web site at http://www.RuthKay.com or E-mail: RuthKay10@aol.com.

Give the Gift of ANATOMY OF A WRINKLE
to Your Loved Ones and Friends

Please Print

Name_____

Organization_____

Address_____

City/State/Zip_____

Phone_____Email_____

❏ YES, I want ____ copies of Anatomy of a Wrinkle at $15.00 each, plus $2.50 shipping (add $1.50 for each additional book). Colorado residents please add $1.02 sales tax per book).

❏ My check or money order for $ _____ is enclosed.

❏ Please charge my ❏ Visa ❏ MasterCard

Card#_____Exp.Date_____

Signature_____

Please make your check payable and return to:

RuthKay Petersen
8547 E. Arapahoe Rd., No. J190
Greenwood Village, CO 80112

Or call your credit card order to: 800-390-1993 or 303 221-7791

Fax: 303 221-7792, E-mail: RuthKay10@aol.com

❏ YES! I would like to receive your newsletter. Please add me to your mailing list.